# THE ANCIENT
# NEAR EAST

# THE ANCIENT NEAR EAST

## An ESSENTIAL GUIDE

John L. McLaughlin

Abingdon Press
Nashville

THE ANCIENT NEAR EAST
AN ESSENTIAL GUIDE

**Library of Congress Cataloging-in-Publication Data**

McLaughlin, John L.
    The ancient Near East : an essential guide / John L. McLaughlin.
       p. cm. — (Essential guides)
    Includes index.
    ISBN 978-1-4267-5327-5 (pbk. : alk. paper) 1. Middle East—History—To 622. I. Title.
    DS62.2.M35 2012
939.4-dc23

                                                                2012033529

12 13 14 15 16 17 18 19 20 21—10 9 8 7 6 5 4 3 2 1
PRINTED IN THE UNITED STATES OF AMERICA

# Contents

Introduction . . . . . . . . . . . . . . . . . . . . . . . . . . . . . . . . . . . . . . . . . xi

Chapter 1: Mesopotamia . . . . . . . . . . . . . . . . . . . . . . . . . . . . . . 1

Chapter 2: Egypt . . . . . . . . . . . . . . . . . . . . . . . . . . . . . . . . . . . . 31

Chapter 3: Hatti . . . . . . . . . . . . . . . . . . . . . . . . . . . . . . . . . . . . 51

Chapter 4: Persia . . . . . . . . . . . . . . . . . . . . . . . . . . . . . . . . . . . 63

Chapter 5: Greece . . . . . . . . . . . . . . . . . . . . . . . . . . . . . . . . . . . 75

Chapter 6: Syro-Palestine . . . . . . . . . . . . . . . . . . . . . . . . . . . . 85

Index of Ancient Texts . . . . . . . . . . . . . . . . . . . . . . . . . . . . . . 127

Index of Names . . . . . . . . . . . . . . . . . . . . . . . . . . . . . . . . . . . 140

Index of Locations . . . . . . . . . . . . . . . . . . . . . . . . . . . . . . . . . 147

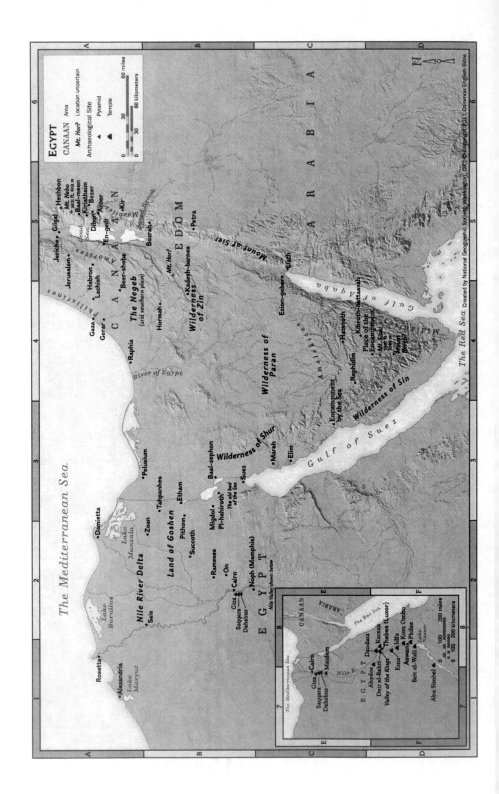

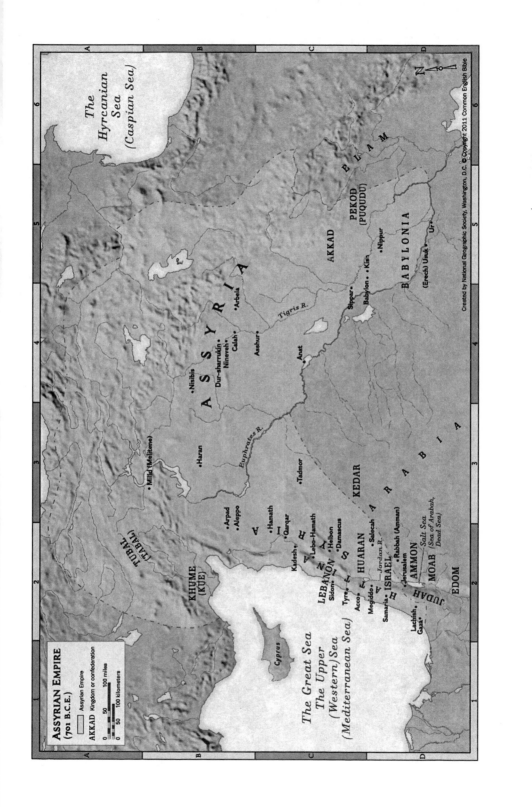

ASSYRIAN EMPIRE
(701 B.C.E.)

Assyrian Empire

AKKAD  Kingdom or confederation

0    50    100 miles
0  50  100 kilometers

The Hyrcanian Sea
(Caspian Sea)

The Great Sea
The Upper
(Western) Sea
(Mediterranean Sea)

Cyprus

TUBAL (TABAL)

KHUME (KÜE)

Kadesh
LEBANON
Sidon
Tyre
Acco
Megiddo
Samaria
ISRAEL
Jerusalem
JUDAH
Lachish
Gaza
AMMON
MOAB
EDOM
Rabbah (Amman)
Salecah
HUARAN
Jordan R.
Salt Sea
(Sea of Arabah,
Dead Sea)

Arpad
Aleppo
Hamath
Qarqar
Lebo-Hamath
Halbon
Damascus

Milid (Melitene)

Haran

Tadmor

KEDAR

ARABIA

Euphrates R.

Nisibis
Dur-sharrukin
Nineveh
Calah
Asshur
Arbela

ASSYRIA

Tigris R.

Anat

AKKAD

ELAM

PEKOD
(PUQUDU)

Sippar
Babylon
Kish
Nippur
(Erech) Uruk
Ur

BABYLONIA

N

Created by National Geographic Society, Washington, D.C. © Copyright 2011 Common English Bible

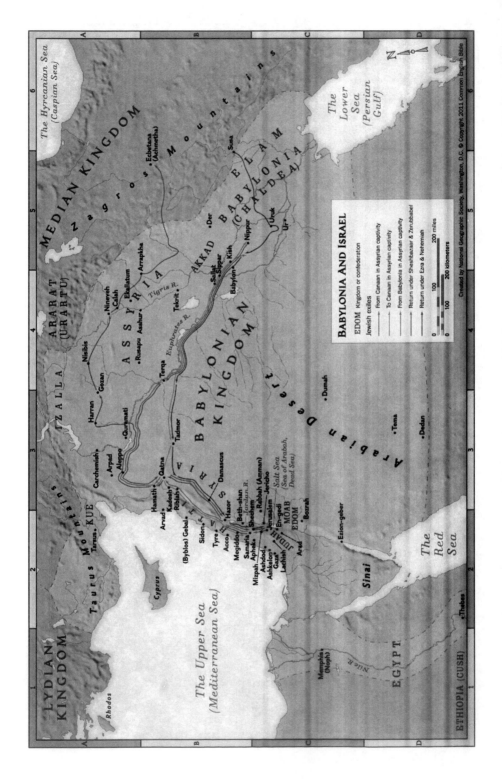

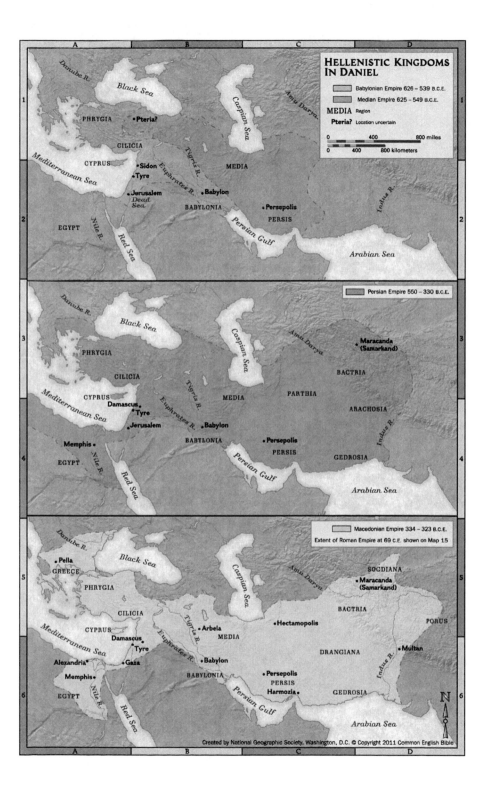

## HELLENISTIC KINGDOMS IN DANIEL

Babylonian Empire 626 – 539 B.C.E.
Median Empire 625 – 549 B.C.E.
MEDIA Region
Pteria? Location uncertain

0     400     800 miles
0     400     800 kilometers

**Map 1**

Danube R.
Black Sea
Caspian Sea
Amu Darya
PHRYGIA
Pteria?
CILICIA
CYPRUS
Mediterranean Sea
Sidon
Tyre
Euphrates R.
Tigris R.
MEDIA
Jerusalem
Dead Sea
Babylon
BABYLONIA
Indus R.
EGYPT
Nile R.
Red Sea
Persian Gulf
Persepolis
PERSIS
Arabian Sea

Persian Empire 550 – 330 B.C.E.

Danube R.
Black Sea
Caspian Sea
Amu Darya
PHRYGIA
Maracanda (Samarkand)
BACTRIA
CILICIA
CYPRUS
Mediterranean Sea
Damascus
Tyre
Tigris R.
MEDIA
PARTHIA
ARACHOSIA
Jerusalem
Euphrates R.
Babylon
Indus R.
Memphis
BABYLONIA
EGYPT
Nile R.
Red Sea
Persepolis
PERSIS
GEDROSIA
Persian Gulf
Arabian Sea

Macedonian Empire 334 – 323 B.C.E.
Extent of Roman Empire at 69 C.E. shown on Map 15

Danube R.
Pella
GREECE
Black Sea
Caspian Sea
Amu Darya
SOGDIANA
PHRYGIA
Maracanda (Samarkand)
BACTRIA
CILICIA
PORUS
CYPRUS
Mediterranean Sea
Damascus
Tyre
Tigris R.
Arbela
MEDIA
Hectamopolis
DRANGIANA
Multan
Alexandria
Gaza
Euphrates R.
Babylon
Indus R.
Memphis
BABYLONIA
Persepolis
PERSIS
EGYPT
Nile R.
Red Sea
Harmozia
Persian Gulf
GEDROSIA
N
Arabian Sea

Created by National Geographic Society, Washington, D.C. © Copyright 2011 Common English Bible

# Introduction

Ancient Israel did not exist in a vacuum. Due to its geographical location between the Mediterranean Sea to the west and the Arabian desert to the east, it formed a land bridge between Egypt and Mesopotamia. Since the trade and military routes ran through Israel, for most of its existence Israel was under the influence, and more often the direct control, of one of those two major powers. This means that the history and literature of the ancient Near East not only provide the general background for understanding the history and literature of ancient Israel, but at times those countries influenced ancient Israel directly, sometimes through their literature, sometimes through their political interactions, and sometimes through both.

This volume examines various countries of the ancient Near East with a view to understanding ancient Israel better. Individual chapters deal with Mesopotamia, Egypt, Hatti (the Hittites), Persia, Greece, and Syro-Palestine. Each chapter outlines the history of the respective area, noting especially any direct interactions with ancient Israel, along with a discussion of relevant literature from the region that helps us understand the First Testament better. In some cases, especially for kingdoms that predate the emergence of Israel itself, this may be a matter of general parallels that illustrate how many aspects of the biblical literature were not unique to ancient Israel but rather part of a larger cultural perspective shared by Israel and its neighbors. Other times, a foreign text might clarify what to us, reading the biblical texts thousands of years later, is an obscure idea or practice but was more commonplace in the ancient world than we know. Finally, sometimes it is possible to demonstrate that individual biblical texts were directly dependent on outside sources, and that recognition provides a fuller understanding of the passage or book. By taking advantage of the insights provided by each of these three approaches to the extrabiblical literature and history, the reader will gain a deeper understanding of the history and literature of ancient Israel itself within its larger context, namely, the ancient Near East.

The way some things are expressed in this book may require an explanation. First, traditional terminology for the two main divisions of the Christian Bible is problematic and has implications for how one interprets both of those sections. *Old Testament* connotes "antiquated," "outdated," and even "replaced" for some. *Hebrew Bible* is popular in many circles, but designating the material by its (primary) language of composition is imprecise because it does not take into account those parts of Daniel and Ezra that were written in Aramaic or the extensive scholarly use of ancient versions in other languages, to say nothing of the second part of the Bible, which still tends to be called the *New Testament*. *Hebrew Bible* also does not incorporate the deuterocanonical books, some written exclusively in Greek, which Roman Catholics and Eastern Orthodox Christians consider scriptural but Protestants and Jews do not. Similarly, *Jewish Bible/Scripture* is inadequate for Christians in general, who consider that collection of books part of their Scriptures. As an uneasy compromise, then, I use the terms *First Testament* and *Second Testament* for the two main divisions of biblical literature.

Second, the abbreviations B.C.E. and, to a far lesser extent, C.E. are used. These stand for "before the Common Era" and "Common Era." They cover the same period as B.C. (before Christ) and A.D. (*anno Domini* = the year of the Lord), but the first set of abbreviations are more commonly used by biblical scholars.

Third, I have handled the replication of ancient Semitic names differently than with individual words. What constitutes a single letter in Semitic languages sometimes requires two Roman letters to convey the equivalent sound, so scholars use a set of diacritical marks that can be added to Western letters to convey such sounds with a single letter as in the original language. Since doing so would make most of the multisyllable names encountered in the following chapters especially confusing for nonspecialists, I have opted to adapt the names to English forms as much as possible so that they will be both recognizable and pronounceable, albeit with difficulty for everyone in some of the more convoluted instances. With respect to the more infrequent citation of specific words, I have employed the full diacritical representation in the interest of precision of expression, but with the hope and expectation that the point being made can be understood by all readers.

Just as ancient Israel did not exist in a vacuum, neither does this book, and I wish to make two acknowledgments. First, those familiar with the field(s) will recognize my dependence on the work of others, both in general and in particular, on almost every page. Unfortunately, the nature of the Essential Guides Series combined with the limitations of space does not allow me to document that dependence through the extensive footnotes that would be required, but I gladly and openly acknowledge my scholarly debt to those who have gone before me. Second, Manda Vrkljan of the John M. Kelly Library at the University of St. Michael's College provided me with the written resources I needed to complete this book. She and her staff in the Kelly InfoExpress Service obtained and delivered articles and books from throughout the physically widespread University of Toronto library system, as well as by Inter-Library Loan from other institutions. Without her constant and cheerful efforts over many months, completing this volume would have been a much more onerous task.

# CHAPTER 1

# Mesopotamia

The region known as Mesopotamia gets its name from two Greek words: *meso* (between) and *potamia* (rivers). This refers to the area between the Tigris River in the east and the Euphrates River in the west, roughly corresponding to modern-day Iraq. During the ancient period, the focus of power and control in the region shifted a number of times between the north and the south. In this chapter, I briefly outline in turn the history of the Third and Second Millennia B.C.E., plus that of the First Millennium up to the conquest of Babylonia by the Persians in 539 B.C.E., along with parallels from the region that shed light on various aspects of the First Testament.

## The Third Millennium

The earliest significant cultural presence in the region was that of the Sumerians. The Sumerians were an Indo-European people who first appeared in the southern part of Mesopotamia in the latter part of the Fourth Millennium B.C.E. They probably originated in India and migrated into the area either along the Persian Gulf or through what is Iran today. They developed the first known system of written language, called *cuneiform*, which gets its name from the use of clusters of wedge (*cuneus* in Latin) shapes to

1

represent sounds. Unlike the modern Western alphabet, in which each character represents a single letter, each cluster represented a syllable or sometimes also an idea (a logogram). Representing all possible combinations of a consonant and a vowel as well as of a vowel and a consonant required a very large number of clusters. In its earliest stage, Sumerian cuneiform had at least one thousand signs, but by the middle of the Third Millennium, this number had been reduced to about six hundred. The Sumerian language itself cannot be linked to any other known language, but the cuneiform writing system was adopted by the Semitic Akkadians of Mesopotamia to represent their own language, after which it evolved into two dialects, namely, Assyrian in the north and Babylonian in the south.

By the late Fourth Millennium, the Sumerians had established a number of city-states in southern Mesopotamia, each of which was ruled by a local priest and exercised control over the immediately surrounding area. By the beginning of the Third Millennium, local control shifted to nonpriestly rulers who passed on their power to their descendants, creating dynasties. Thus, this stage of Sumerian history is known as the Early Dynastic period and spans approximately 2900–2350 B.C.E. At times the individual city-states were independent from each other while at other periods one city-state would expand its control over its neighbors, such that the latter served as vassals to the dominant city. The cities of Kish, Uruk, Ur, and Lagash each in turn served as the center of a Sumerian kingdom that incorporated most, if not all, of southern Mesopotamia.

Around 2350 B.C.E., control of the region passed to Semites living in the area when Sharru-kin (legitimate king), better known as Sargon, overthrew the Sumerians and established the Akkadian Empire, named after its capital city of Akkad. Sargon launched military campaigns to incorporate northern Mesopotamia into his empire, followed by raids westward as far as the Mediterranean Sea. Sargon's sons Rimush (2278–2270 B.C.E.) and Manishtushu (2269–2255 B.C.E.) faced attacks from within and without, respectively, but Sargon's grandson, Naram-sin (2254–2218 B.C.E.), solidified Akkadian power throughout Mesopotamia. Naram-sin's own son Shar-kali-sharri (2217–2193 B.C.E.) maintained Akkadian control of the region, but after his reign the kingdom entered a period of weakness until its eventual collapse (ca. 2154 B.C.E.). It is uncertain whether this collapse was solely the result of internal disarray or was completed by attacks by the Gutians, invaders from the Zagros Mountains to the east, but in any case the Gutians subsequently dominated the region for about a century. However, they had neither the interest nor the ability to establish a stable central government, and this period was described in later literature as one of barbarity, cruelty, and confusion. Eventually, Utu-kegal succeeded in driving out the Gutians, ushering in the Third Ur Dynasty, which lasted from 2112 to 2004 B.C.E. Although this period is sometimes described as a resurgence of Sumerian power, by this point the Sumerian and Semitic populations of Mesopotamia had become intertwined. As such, it is more correct to speak of a renaissance of Sumerian culture than of the Sumerians replacing the Akkadians and their kin.

Since the Sumerians and Akkadians predate the Israelites by at least a thousand years, it would be anachronistic to speak of any direct influence from the earliest Mesopotamians on the history or literature of the later biblical period. However, some similarities show the larger cultural context for the biblical literature itself, demonstrating that some of its concerns were already shared by much earlier people. This is most obvious in the extensive Sumerian wisdom tradition, which included proverbs, didactic tales, disputations, word lists, fables, and so on, all of which are paralleled in the Bible. In addition, in the Sumerian schools the teacher was called "father" and the student was called "son," terminology that is repeated a number of times in the opening chapters of Proverbs (e.g., 1:8, 10, 15; 2:1; 3:1, 11, 21; 4:1, 10; 5:1, 7; 6:1, 3, 20; 7:1; see also 23:19, 25, 26; 24:13, 21; 27:11). This shows that the Israelites' search for insight into the world around them, especially as reflected in human experience, was not unique to Israel, as we will see more than once in dealing with other nations as well.

In addition to this general similarity concerning how both ancient Israel and ancient Mesopotamia sought to acquire wisdom and communicate it, the content of the Sumerian work *A Man and His God* shows some affinity with the situation of Job in the Bible. A man who had been prosperous and healthy is afflicted and then scorned by his friends. However, unlike Job's protestations of innocence, the Sumerian concludes that all humans are inherently

3

sinful, and so he asks for forgiveness, just as Job's friends encourage him to do. He addresses his personal god (cf. Job's hope for an advocate in Job 9:33; 19:25), and his situation is reversed.

Another parallel between Sumerian and biblical texts is the concept of a universal flood, although only part of the Sumerian story has been discovered. After narrating the divine decision to cause a flood and how one of the gods warns the human Ziusudra, the text breaks off; when it resumes, the flood has lasted seven days and nights, after which Ziusudra sacrifices to the gods (cf. Gen 8:20). The damaged nature of the Sumerian tablets prevents the closer comparison to the Noah story that is possible with the later Babylonian-period material (see further below). Nonetheless, the Mesopotamian King List attributes great age to the kings who ruled prior to the flood, with the reigns of the earliest Sumerian kings of up to 62,000 years far outstripping the 969-year life span of Methuselah, the oldest man in the Bible (Gen 5:27). Nevertheless, there is a shared view that the flood marks a dividing line in terms of the length of human life, although in the Bible, God announces a shorter human life span just before the flood (Gen 6:3). In addition, according to *Enmerkar and the Lord of Aratta*, all humans spoke a single language until Enki (Ea) introduced diverse tongues, which parallels how Yahweh confused the tongues of those building the tower of Babel (Genesis 11).

Traditions connected with the birth of Sargon are reflected in the story of Moses. Sargon was born in secret to a priestess, put into the river in a basket of rushes, and rescued by a water drawer named Akki; later, the goddess Ishtar elevated Sargon to the throne. Similarly, Moses was born in secret and set adrift in a basket on the Nile River, only to be discovered by an Egyptian princess and raised as her own son. Moses eventually left Egypt but was called by Yahweh to lead the Israelites out of Egypt. The parallels are clear, but not unique to these two individuals. There are also similarities to the story of Romulus and Remus, the founders of Rome, who were also born to a priestess and set adrift, only to be found by a she-wolf and then raised by a shepherd. It is difficult to say whether there is any direct influence among the three versions or simply a common tradition, but the latter does not lessen the fact that the details of Moses' birth were not unique in the ancient world.

Another interesting parallel from this period can be found in *The Curse of Agade* (i.e., Akkad). As part of his political and military expansion, Naram-sin sacked the city of Nippur, during which he defiled Enlil's sanctuary there. According to *The Curse of Agade*, in response to this sacrilege eight major deities supported the chief of the pantheon by withdrawing their protection of Akkad itself and bringing the Gutians into the land as punishment for Naram-sin's offense. This explanation of military defeat and subjugation as the consequence for earlier sins corresponds to the frequent biblical theme in the books of Judges, Samuel, and Kings that Yahweh uses other nations to punish Israel's apostasy, culminating in the explanation for the Babylonian destruction of Jerusalem and the Temple in 587 B.C.E. that is found in Kings, Jeremiah, and Ezekiel. Related to this are the *Laments* over the destruction of Ur, Sumer, Nippur, Eridu, and Uruk, which are similar to the book of Lamentations and portions of Jeremiah and Ezekiel, which mourn the destruction of Jerusalem at the hands of the Babylonian army.

Many kinds of Mesopotamian divination are paralleled in the Bible. These are attempts to determine the divine will for a given situation through the mechanical manipulation of physical elements. The most common Mesopotamian approach was the examination of the liver of sacrificed animals by the *baru* priests, who compared them to clay models with inscriptions; the model that best approximated the shape, size, color, and so forth of the actual liver indicated the gods' message. Although this is not reflected in the First Testament, some liver models have been found at Hazor in northern Israel.

Other Mesopotamian methods of divination include mixing water and oil (cf. Gen 44:5), taking the casual comments of others as indicating a course of action (e.g., 1 Sam 14:9-10; 1 Kings 20:32-33), interpreting dreams (especially Joseph and Daniel), and casting lots. Casting lots is explicitly stated as the means of selecting the "scapegoat" (Lev 16:8), dividing the land (Josh 18:6), selecting Saul as the first king of Israel (1 Sam 10:20-21), and determining guard duties (1 Chron 26:13), among other things, and is probably the way Achan is identified as the one who did not dedicate the spoils of war to Yahweh (Joshua 7). The Urim and Thummim, which were probably different colored balls signifying yes and no, were used in a similar way: Saul invoked them as the way of determining who violated his oath that no one would eat before evening (1 Sam 14:24-42, especially v. 41), and this is the best interpretation of the priestly use of the Urim and Thummim in some instances (Num 27:21; 1 Sam 28:6; Ezra 2:63; Neh 7:65; and almost certainly Exod 28:30; Lev 8:8; and Deut 33:8). In all these methods of seeking guidance from the heavenly realm, the expectation is that God (or the gods) guides the process.

Finally, we can note Mesopotamian texts from the end of the Third Millennium B.C.E. that describe occasional royal amnesties, in which a king would cancel debts as well as any enslavement that may have resulted from them. The parallel to the Jubilee Year in Lev 25:8-17, in which all debts are forgiven and all slaves set free, is obvious, although there are differences, namely, that the Mesopotamian amnesty is initiated at the option of the king, usually upon his assuming the throne or celebrating a long reign, whereas the biblical law mandates that this be done every fifty years. Nonetheless, the Hebrew word for "liberty" in Lev 25:10 (*děrôr*) is cognate with *durāru* found in the Mesopotamian texts.

## The Second Millennium

Following the collapse of the Third Ur Dynasty at the end of the Third Millennium B.C.E., the Amorites dominated southern Mesopotamia, ushering in what is known as the Old Babylonian period (ca. 2003–1595 B.C.E.). These Semitic peoples get their name from the Akkadian word *amurru*, which means "westerner," thus indicating their probable origins in what is now modern Syria. First mentioned in Sumerian texts (as *MAR.TU*) from the middle of the Third Millennium, they were migrating across the Euphrates by the end of that Millennium in ever increasing numbers, leading the king of Ur to build a wall to keep them out. The barrier proved unsuccessful, and together with the encroaching Elamites from the east, the Amorites contributed to the downfall of Ur. At first, the Amorites established a number of smaller kingdoms, but these eventually came under the authority of either of the rival cities of Isin or Larsa.

Meanwhile, in northern Mesopotamia King Naram-sin of Eshnunna exerted power over the region, in the course of which he captured the city of Ashshur. However, that city was soon conquered by Shamshi-Adad I, who extended his control farther northwest, annexing Mari and sending his armies as far west as modern Lebanon, thereby establishing the first, but short-lived, Assyrian Empire. He divided his territory between his two sons, but they were unable to maintain control over the region, falling prey to the Babylonians in the south. Babylon had emerged as a small city-state around 1894 B.C.E., but its first five kings played minor roles in southern Mesopotamia. However, that changed after Hammurabi came to the throne in 1792 B.C.E. For the first decade or so he focused on solidifying his power both internally in Babylon and externally by annexing nearby cities, followed by eighteen years consolidating his control over both aspects of his kingdom. Then, he began to expand his power, conquering in turn the Elamite invaders from the east (1764 B.C.E.), the kingdom of Larsa to the south (1763 B.C.E.), the important city-state of Mari (1761 B.C.E.), and the now weakened Assyria to the north (1756 B.C.E.), thus establishing the first (Old) Babylonian Empire.

In keeping with an established pattern, this empire did not long survive his death, and the conquered territories gradually slipped away from his successors, although his dynasty survived in the capital city of Babylon until the Hittites sacked it in 1595 B.C.E., only to withdraw immediately to their homeland (cf. Chapter 3). After the Hittites left, the city of Babylon fell to the Kassites, invaders from the east, who went on to rule southern Mesopotamia for 435 years, although often subservient to Assyria in the north, until defeated by raiding Elamites in 1158 B.C.E. Little is known of their rule, other than that it was characterized by the restoration of Babylonia's infrastructure and preservation of its culture. The Kassites assimilated with their subjects and left no records in their native language. They were followed by the Second Dynasty of Isin, which ruled Babylonia from 1158 to 1027 B.C.E.

Meanwhile, Assyria regained its independence from Babylonia following Hammurabi's death and, after about thirty years of civil war, established a stable presence in northern Mesopotamia for the next two hundred years. They lived undisturbed by their neighbors until Mitanni, a Hurrian kingdom in northern Syria and southeast Anatolia (see Chapter 6), made Assyria its vassal at the beginning of the Fifteenth Century B.C.E. This situation lasted to varying degrees for about 150 years until the reign of Ashur-uballit I (1365–1330 B.C.E.), who took advantage of Hittite encroachment on Mitanni from the west to throw off Mitanni's shackles, thus beginning Assyria's return to regional domination. Shalmaneser I (ca. 1273–1244 B.C.E.) eventually conquered Mitanni itself and, along with his successor Tukulti-Ninurta I (ca. 1243–1207 B.C.E.), expanded Assyrian territory, including portions of Kassite Babylonia to the south. However, in the Twelfth Century B.C.E. the ancient world from the Mediterranean to Mesopotamia experienced a major societal collapse, brought on by massive and extended drought, with the Hittite empire collapsing and Egypt and Assyria entering a period of weakness. This upheaval was reinforced by major migrations throughout the area, including the Sea Peoples marching through the Hittite Empire, destroying Ugarit, and eventually being repulsed by Egypt, while at the same time the Arameans of northern Syria encroached on Mesopotamia. Although Assyria managed to keep from being overrun, its imperial aspirations were checked until the middle of the Tenth Century B.C.E., at which point it would rise again to expand relentlessly westward.

As with the Third Millennium, there are Mesopotamian compositions from the Second Millennium that parallel elements of biblical literature. In contrast to the Third Millennium literature, however, there are also indications that some of these may have directly influenced the biblical texts in more than one area. The first of these is related to creation. For instance, some general parallels can be seen between the Babylonian work *Enuma Elish* (from the text's opening words, meaning "When on high") and the creation story in Genesis 1. In *Enuma Elish*, the god Marduk defeats the sea goddess, Tiamat, cuts her body in half, and uses the two portions to make the earth and the sky. This compares with Yahweh's division of the primeval waters into those above and below, a point reinforced by the Hebrew word *tĕhôm* translated as "deep" (Gen 1:2), which is cognate with Tiamat. In *Enuma Elish* the sun, the moon, and the heavenly bodies are also created to mark the passage of time, just as in Gen 1:14.

Nevertheless, there are important differences between the Babylonian and biblical creation stories as well. Most important, God creates the world by speaking rather than through undertaking divine battle, and in *Enuma Elish* humans are created from the blood of Tiamat's henchman, Kingu, in order to assume the role of the minor deities in providing food and drink to the larger pantheon, whereas according to Gen 1:26 humans are created in the divine image in order to have dominion over the earth. Thus, while the biblical authors may have known of the Babylonian creation myth as a result of Mesopotamian control over Israel and Judah during the First Millennium, and especially during the Babylonian exile, they altered it in significant ways to present a different understanding of both God and creation.

Similarities are also evident between Mesopotamian flood stories and the Noah story in Genesis 6–9. The *Epic of Atrahasis* (Eighteenth Century B.C.E.) includes a creation story similar to that in *Enuma Elish*, in which the blood of a dead god is mixed with clay figures to produce humans, who once again are created to provide for the gods. It goes on to narrate how they became so numerous on the earth that the noise keeps the chief deity Enlil awake. After plague and drought fail to reduce the population enough, he decides to send a flood to eliminate them completely. However, Enki, the god of wisdom, tells Atrahasis to build a boat, roofed over and sealed with pitch, which Atrahasis and his family enter. The text breaks off at that point and the flood itself is not narrated, but when the text resumes, Atrahasis offers a sacrifice to the gods and a different means of population control is devised.

The Atrahasis story was copied and expanded into the later Epic of Gilgamesh, where it has even closer points of contact with the biblical story. In the Gilgamesh version, the hero is Utnapishtim, who is told by Ea to build a seven-story cubed boat from reeds, onto which he takes his family and various animals. After seven days, the boat runs aground on a mountaintop, and Utnapishtim sends out a dove, then a swallow, then a raven. The first two return, but the third does not, so he releases the animals and offers a sacrifice to the gods who, having grown hungry due to the absence of humans to feed them, flock around it "like flies." While some details differ between this and the Noah story, such as the boat's dimensions and construction material, the length of the flood, the exact animals onboard, and the specific birds sent out, the similarities are striking. In particular, both stories mention three birds after the flood, the third of which does not return, thereby indicating that the waters had receded, and two of them are the same, namely, a dove and a raven. In addition, the word for "pitch" (*kōper*) in Genesis 6:14 does not occur elsewhere in the Bible, but its Akkadian equivalent, *kupru*, is found in the Mesopotamian flood stories. Add the fact that widespread flooding was common in the flat river plains of Mesopotamia but not in the more hilly Israel, and it is likely that the Israelite authors knew the Mesopotamian myths and used them for their own purposes. But just as with the creation traditions, they altered them to present a different understanding of God, in that Yahweh brings the flood as punishment for universal sin rather than simply to eliminate noisy humans, and Yahweh reacts to Noah's sacrifice not like a hungry fly but rather in a more dignified manner by simply smelling "the pleasing odor" (Gen 8:21).

Another area in which there are parallels between Mesopotamia in this period and biblical materials is that of law. Once again, there are similarities on both the general and the specific levels. In terms of general format, most of the stipulations in the existing Mesopotamian law codes are expressed in terms of specific cases, namely, if X happens, then Y is the result, or someone who does X shall experience Y consequences. Such *casuistic* or case laws are also found in the Bible, although the similarity might just be the result of common legal traditions. However, the shared casuistic formulation is highlighted by the presence in the biblical material of *apodictic* laws, that is, direct commands in the form of "you shall" or prohibitions in the form of "you shall not." Apodictic laws are found in the Ten Commandments and frequently elsewhere in Exodus, Numbers, and Leviticus, but this form is rarely found in the Mesopotamian material.

There are also parallels between the two legal traditions in terms of actual content. For instance, Exod 21:35 states, "If someone's ox hurts the ox of another, so that it dies, then they shall sell the live ox and divide the price of it; and the dead animal they shall also divide." This is strikingly similar to a law from Eshnunna in the Nineteenth Century B.C.E.: "If an ox gored and killed an ox, both ox owners shall divide the price of the live ox and the carcass of the dead ox." Granted, there is no evidence of a direct connection from the Laws of Eshnunna to the book of Exodus at least one thousand years later for just this law and one other concerning burglary, and it is entirely possible that diverse people could develop such similar laws independently of each other. However, the very close wording in both cases suggests at least a common tradition from which both drew. Similarly, a Middle Assyrian law (ca. Fourteenth Century B.C.E.) allows a father-in-law to give his son's widow without children to another son, just as in Genesis 38 and Deut 25:5-10 (cf. Ruth 4).

A stronger case can be made that the Covenant Code in Exodus 20:23–23:19 draws more directly from the famous Code of Hammurabi, compiled about a century after that of Eshnunna. This section of Exodus consists of two sets of apodictic laws (Exod 20:23-26; 22:17–23:19) surrounding a series of casuistic laws (Exod 21:2–22:16), just as Hammurabi's Code consists of casuistic laws surrounded by a prologue and an epilogue. Not only that, but there are points of contact between Hammurabi's prologue and epilogue and the Covenant Code's apodictic laws, in terms of both content and sequence, the strongest being a common concern for the weak, orphaned, and widow in Hammurabi and the foreigner, widow, and orphaned in Exod 22:20-23. Moreover, the central casuistic laws of the Covenant Code include fourteen topics that are found in Hammurabi's Code as well, with comparable wording and mostly in the same sequence. Both points can be seen in the laws concerning a goring ox:

| Exodus 21:28-32 | Hammurabi Laws 250-52 |
|---|---|
| [28]When an ox gores a man or a woman to death, the ox shall be stoned, and its flesh shall not be eaten; but the owner of the ox shall not be liable. | [250]If an ox gores a man while passing through the street and kills, that case has no claim. |
| [29]If the ox has been accustomed to gore in the past, and its owner has been warned but has not restrained it, and it kills a man or a woman, the ox shall be stoned, and its owner | [251]If a man's ox is a habitual gorer, and his district has informed him that it is a habitual gorer, but he did not file its horns and did not control his ox, and that |

also shall be put to death. [30]If a ransom is imposed on the owner, then the owner shall pay whatever is imposed for the redemption of the victim's life.

[31]If it gores a boy or a girl, the owner shall be dealt with according to this same rule.

[32]If the ox gores a male or female slave, the owner shall pay to the slaveowner thirty shekels of silver, and the ox shall be stoned.

ox gores someone, he shall pay one-half *mina* (= thirty shekels) of silver.

[252]If it is the slave of a free person, he shall pay one-third mina (= twenty shekels) of silver.

As the comparison above shows, the biblical text sometimes includes additional laws, usually for the sake of completeness. Yet it sometimes omits laws found in Hammurabi's Code as secondary to the overall purpose while also occasionally altering the sequence found in Hammurabi's Code in order to draw better connections. Nevertheless, when taken all together, the preceding evidence indicates that the Covenant Code has directly and intentionally drawn upon Hammurabi's Code. This does not mean that the two date from the same time, however, since the biblical writers could easily have encountered the latter while later subject to either the Assyrian or the Babylonian Empire during the First Millennium.

Another area for comparison is that of Wisdom literature. Throughout the Second Millennium, the various Mesopotamian cultures continued to collect proverbs, fables, moralistic stories, and so on. The Epic of Gilgamesh in particular contains two pieces of advice similar to ones found in Qoheleth (Ecclesiastes). One is a proverb that compares the strength of two individuals as greater than either alone, just like a doubled cord. This can be compared with Qoh 4:9-12:

Better two than one, for whom there are better wages for their labor.

12

For if either should fall, the one can raise his comrade.
But woe to him, the one who falls with no second to raise
him.
Also, if two lie down they are warm.
But as for one, how can he become warm?
Even if a single one can overcome him
The two can stand against him.
The threefold cord cannot be broken in a hurry.

Elsewhere, Gilgamesh is encouraged to enjoy life, with the passage mentioning food, clothes, washed hair, and the company of one's wife as part of human destiny. In addition to Qoheleth's frequent exhortations to enjoy food, drink, and pleasure in general (2:24; 3:12-13, 22; 5:17-18; 8:15; cf. 11:9), the things mentioned in Gilgamesh appear together in Qoh 9:7-9:

> Go, eat with joy your bread.
> Drink with a good heart your wine,
> For God has already accepted your works.
> At all time let your garments be white.
> Oil upon your head do not let it be lacking.
> Enjoy life with the woman whom you love
> All your empty days,
> Which he has given to you under the sun,
> All the days of your absurdity.
> For that is your lot in life and in your toil
> At which you toil under the sun.

In both cases the actual wording is different enough to indicate that these are not cases of direct borrowing from one to the other, but they do show that Israel's reflection upon the human situation at times led to insights that were anticipated by their Mesopotamian predecessors.

Similarly, two works as a whole from near the end of the period are worth mentioning in relationship to the book of Job. The Poem of the Righteous Sufferer, known by its opening words as "I Will Praise the Lord of Wisdom" (*ludlul bēl nēmeqi*), deals with an individual who experiences undeserved suffering, just as Job did. If that individual, named Shubshi-meshre-Shakkan in the text, is to

13

be identified with a Kassite official known to have existed around 1292 B.C.E., then the text could date from then or soon after. This person is struck by disease, mocked by his friends, and alienated from family, and when the usual sacrifices and comparable rituals bring no relief, he feels that he has been abandoned by his gods, his angel, and his protective spirit. The similarities to Job's situation, allowing for differences due to Israelite religious beliefs, are certainly striking. But at the same time there are differences. For instance, Shubshi-meshre-Shakkan's suffering is described in great, painful detail, while in comparison Job has a mere rash. At the same time, whereas Job protests his innocence throughout, Shubshi-meshre-Shakkan believes he must have committed some sin, even if inadvertently, and so does not blame Marduk, at least not directly, and in the end he repents and is restored to health.

Another work from the same period that deals with questions of human suffering and divine justice is *The Babylonian Theodicy*. The author, Saggil-kinam-ubbib, was a sage under Nebuchadnezzar I, which would date the work to the period 1124–1103 B.C.E. Just as Job discusses his situation with his three friends, this piece contains a dialogue between a man and a friend in which the former presents instances of injustice, beginning with his own, while the friend tries to assert traditional doctrines. After much discussion the friend admits that humans are perverse because the gods made them so. Much like the book of Job, this text identifies the problem of human suffering but does not solve it. Once again, these similarities do not require dependence or even knowledge, but they do illustrate that ancient Israelite questions about theodicy were not unique to them.

There are also minor points of contact between Mesopotamia and biblical rituals. One is the determination of an individual's destiny at the New Year in both cultures. At the Babylonian New Year *akītu* festival, fates for the coming year were written on the Tablet of Destinies, which was then sealed with the Seal of Destinies. This is reflected in the discussions in heaven about Job's fate that take place "on that day" (Job 1:6; 2:1, author's translation), as well as the hardening of hearts in Isa 6:9-10, and was expanded in later Jewish traditions where the events of an individual's coming year are written down in the Book of Life on Rosh

Hashanah (the New Year), with the Book then closed ten days later on Yom Kippur (the Day of Atonement). The annual scapegoat ritual was mandated for Yom Kippur, in which Aaron symbolically transferred the sins of the people onto a goat that was then driven into the wilderness "to Azazel" (Lev 16:8-10, 21-22), a name that occurs in an Akkadian text from the Eighteenth Century B.C.E. found at Alalakh in Syria (see also Chapter 3).

We can also quickly note references to various other Mesopotamian deities in the Bible. The references to Sakkuth and Kaiwan in Amos 5:26 reflect a title of the hunter deity Ninurta and the Babylonian name for the planet Saturn, respectively. Isaiah 34:14 refers to "Lilith" (thus the New Revised Standard Version; the Revised Standard Version translates this as "night hag" while the King James Version renders it as "screech owl"), a Mesopotamian desert demon. Later Jewish tradition considered her to be Adam's first wife, before Eve, who was rejected because she would not submit to her husband and subsequently became a demonic figure, who attacked pregnant women to steal their children and tried to seduce single males. Similarly, Gen 4:7 is often translated as "sin is lurking at the door" (NRSV), but the Hebrew here (*rōbēṣ*, which can be translated as either "crouching" or "a croucher" at the door) matches Mesopotamian *rābiṣu*, a demon that guards doorways, suggesting the second translation of the Hebrew term.

More significantly, the passing reference in Ezek 8:14 to women weeping for Tammuz in the Temple area reflects the Sumerian myth of Dumuzi descending to the underworld, which was memorialized by ritual mourning in Assyrian contexts. One of the months in the Jewish calendar is still called Tammuz and includes fasting and lament on the seventeenth day, now explained as marking the Babylonians' breaching of Jerusalem's walls. We also gain insight into the biblical cherubim (*kĕrûbîm*) from the Assyrian *keribu*. The latter were hybrid beings with a human head, an animal's body (most commonly a lion or bull), and an eagle's wings. Statues of these creatures standing as tall as eighteen feet guarded the entrances to temples and palaces, just as in the Bible cherubim stood guard at the entrance to the garden of Eden (Gen 3:24), inside the Holy of Holies in the Jerusalem temple (Exod 25:18-20; 1 Kings 6:23-28), and beneath the divine throne

(Ezekiel 1). They also escorted the "glory of the LORD" when it left Jerusalem (Ezek 10:18-19).

# The First Millennium

After a period in which it was focused inward, maintaining its borders against foreign incursions, Assyria began to assert control over the surrounding territory again in the last part of the Tenth Century B.C.E. With each successive king, its armies expanded the empire, dominating Babylonia to the south and, most important for our purposes, gradually extending westward toward the Mediterranean Sea. Eventually, this military encroachment affected Israel, starting in the middle of the Ninth Century B.C.E. In response to the westward campaigns of Shalmaneser III (858–824 B.C.E.), the Arameans (in modern-day Syria) organized a coalition of neighboring countries to oppose the Assyrians. This included northern Israel ruled by King Ahab who, according to Assyrian records, contributed two thousand chariots and ten thousand soldiers. The opposing armies met in 853 B.C.E. at Qarqar on the Orontes River, and although Shalmaneser claimed victory, he still faced opposition in this area. Eventually, however, he was able to overcome the Aramean capital of Damascus and set up a stele on Mount Carmel on the northern Mediterranean coast of Israel to mark the southern extent of his authority; he received tribute from Tyre and Sidon in Phoenicia and from King Jehu of Israel. His Black Obelisk records a number of items that he received from King Jehu and includes a picture of the Israelite king bowing before him.

However, upon Shalmaneser's death and for almost eighty years afterward, the Assyrians were preoccupied with the kingdom of Urartu to their north, leaving the area to their west alone and thus allowing for a period of peace and economic prosperity in Israel and among its neighbors. This is reflected in the growth of an upper-class elite during the reign of Jeroboam II (ca. 786–746 B.C.E.), accompanied by extreme social inequality that was condemned by the prophet Amos.

Israel's political independence ended with the ascension of Tiglath-pileser III (744–727 B.C.E.) to the throne. He drove the

Urartians out of Assyrian territory and invaded both their home-land and the regions in northern Syria that they controlled. At the same time, he sought positive relations with Babylonia to his south, but after being forced to suppress a rebellion there, he installed himself on the Babylonian throne, unifying the northern and southern regions of Mesopotamia into a single political entity. This led to the smaller states to the southwest of Mesopotamia, including Israel, submitting to Assyrian authority: 2 Kings 15:19-21 describes King Menahem of Israel paying Tiglath-pileser III (called Pul in the Bible) one thousand silver talents in order to retain his throne. As a result, when Tiglath-pileser marched against Gaza in 734 B.C.E., he was able to pass through the region without opposition. However, the following year Rezin of Damascus formed a coalition with his neighbors, including Pekah of Israel, against Assyria. According to 2 Kings 16:5-9 (see also Isaiah 7–8), they invaded Judah when King Ahaz refused to join them, planning to replace him with someone who would support them. Ahaz appealed to Tiglath-pileser III, accompanied by gold and silver, and the Assyrian emperor succeeded in destroying Damascus and annexing portions of Israel, such as Gilead and Galilee, within a year. While Ahaz served Assyria as a loyal vassal in the following years, Israel to the north continued to resist Assyrian control.

Tiglath-pileser III was followed by Shalmaneser V, whose five-year reign included the conquest of the northern Israelite capital of Samaria at about the same time that the Assyrian throne was being seized by Sargon II (721–705 B.C.E.). It fell to Sargon to complete the punishment by making Samaria an Assyrian province, scattering a large part of the Israelite population throughout the Assyrian Empire while simultaneously importing others from throughout the empire. This common Assyrian policy was intended to undermine the ties of both groups to their homelands with the goal of reducing possible revolts. In 2 Kings 17:24 we read of people being imported from "Babylon, Cuthah, Avva, Hamath, and Sepharvaim," although extant Assyrian texts mention only Arabs. The biblical text says that these foreigners were settled "in place of the people of Israel," but the reality is that they intermingled with the remaining Israelites, constituting the Samarians of later texts and the Samaritans mentioned in the

17

Second Testament Gospels. In 712 B.C.E. Sargon II subdued Philistia along the coast, expelling Hezekiah from the region (cf. his Azekah Tablet and 2 Kings 18:7-8), and established a garrison on the Egyptian border. Closer to home, the Chaldean (southeast Mesopotamia) Marduk-apla-iddina II seized the Babylonian throne upon Sargon II's ascension in the north, but twelve years later Sargon drove him out and was himself crowned king of Babylon.

Sargon was followed in 705 B.C.E. by his son Sennacherib, whose attention was quickly drawn to Babylonia, where Marduk-apla-iddina II once again seized the throne for nine months (703–702 B.C.E.). The latter sought allies throughout the Assyrian Empire, including Judah, and 2 Kings 20:12 and Isa 39:1 (where he is called Merodach-baladan) mention envoys he sent to King Hezekiah of Judah. Hezekiah took advantage of the situation in Mesopotamia to withdraw his allegiance to the Assyrians, relying in part on a new alliance with the Egyptians and Ethiopians. In preparation for the expected Assyrian army, Hezekiah arranged for a tunnel to be dug from Jerusalem's main water source at the Gihon spring outside the city walls through to the pool of Siloam (2 Kings 20:20) to ensure a constant supply during siege. An inscription found in the tunnel in 1838 C.E. and now housed in the Istanbul Archaeology Museum describes how two teams dug from either end and met in the middle. The "broad wall" uncovered in the current old city of Jerusalem can also be dated to this period. The wall, some 7 meters wide and at least 3.3 meters high, formed part of the city's western defenses; Isaiah 22:10 may be criticizing its construction at the expense of individual homes (cf. Neh 3:8).

Once Sennacherib had dealt with the Babylonian revolt, driving the usurper into Elam, he turned his attention to the west. According to the Prism of Sennacherib (parallel accounts are found in the Taylor Prism and the Jerusalem Prism), he defeated a combined army of Egyptians and Ethiopians at Eltekeh in the coastal plain, on his way to Jerusalem. He then laid siege to Lachish, which guarded the approaches to the capital. While 2 Kings 18:13-14 mentions it just as one of the "fortified cities of Judah" that Sennacherib captured, we can gather much greater detail from Assyrian records. Sennacherib's Prism boasts of how he captured forty-six "strong, walled cities" plus smaller towns in Judah through the use of "battering-rams and by bringing up siege-engines, and by attacking and storming on foot, by mines, tunnels, and breaches," while also noting a large number of captives (200,150) and livestock as spoils of war. A relief from Sennacherib's palace at Nineveh depicts the siege of Lachish in particular, with siege ramps and battering rams and a parade of captives past the city's leaders who are being skinned alive. The intensity of the attack is confirmed by archaeological remains, which include a stone-and-dirt ramp against the city wall that would facilitate the use of battering rams and siege towers, hundreds of Assyrian arrowheads on the ramp and the city wall, and nearly fifteen hundred skulls in a cave nearby.

In the Prism, Sennacherib goes on to describe a similar siege of Jerusalem but does not say that he conquered the city. Instead, he claims only that he shut Hezekiah up "like a bird in a cage" prior to receiving tribute from him, and it is highly unlikely that Sennacherib would fail to mention capturing the city if he actually had. Sennacherib's account is consistent with the biblical claim that the city was not overcome, as well as the reference in 2 Kings 18:14-16 to Hezekiah's payment of tribute to get Sennacherib to withdraw. However, 2 Kings 18 goes on to narrate a subsequent siege of Jerusalem under the leadership of the Tartan, the Rabsaris, and the Rabshakeh, three Assyrian officials. Then, 2 Kings 19:9 notes that Sennacherib heard that "King Tirhakah of Ethiopia . . . has set out to fight against you," but this force is not mentioned again. Sennacherib may actually have withdrawn in the face of a fresh army led by Taharqa, who at that time was a general but would go on to assume the Egyptian throne in 690 B.C.E. Second Kings 19:35-36 says that Sennacherib returned home after the angel of the Lord struck dead 185,000 Assyrians overnight. The latter event is often interpreted as the result of sudden disease ravaging the Assyrian soldiers.

The Greek historian Herodotus presents yet another version of events that echoes the last two possibilities by combining an Egyptian army with divine intervention. In his *Histories* 2.141 (ca. 450 B.C.E.) Herodotus narrates that as Sennacherib faced an otherwise unknown Egyptian king named Sethos (perhaps Taharqa's priestly title?), the latter prayed to his gods, who sent mice into the Assyrian camp to chew through their quivers, bowstrings, and thongs on their shields, rendering them unable to wield their weapons and resulting in their overwhelming defeat. Some explain the discrepancies among these variant versions by positing a second Assyrian campaign (ca. 689 B.C.E.) when Hezekiah rebelled a second time, but was saved by Taharqa's intervention, although there is no reference to a second rebellion in any Assyrian records. In any case, however these variant traditions are to be reconciled, it is clear from history that after this, Hezekiah was once again an obedient Assyrian vassal.

Sennacherib was killed by one or more of his sons in 681 B.C.E. because he had destroyed Babylon eight years earlier. Assyrian documents name only Arda-Mulissi while 2 Kings 19:37 implicates Adrammelech (a possible corruption of Arda-Mulissi) and Sharezer. Sennacherib was followed by another son, Esarhaddon, who reigned until 669 B.C.E. In addition to military campaigns subduing lands north and east of Assyria, he put down rebellions in the west, including Sidon in 677 B.C.E.; he shared the spoils with his ally in the battle, the king of Tyre, and a treaty from this event mentions Judah as one of numerous other Assyrian allies in the area, a situation that prevailed throughout Esarhaddon's rule. He invaded Egypt in 671 B.C.E., capturing the capital city Memphis, driving Pharaoh Taharqa into Upper Egypt, and installing a garrison in the land. The Egyptians continued to resist Assyrian rule, however, requiring that the latter return in force on more than one occasion.

Among the interesting literary artifacts from Esarhaddon's rule are requests for guidance on military affairs from the king to the gods. After making inquiries about whether he should embark on specific military campaigns, Esarhaddon receives oracular responses from the gods urging him to go forward, confident that they will be with him. This parallels comparable episodes in the Bible, such as David asking whether he should attack the Philistines (2 Sam 5:19-20) and the king of Israel asking whether he should go up against Ramoth-Gilead (1 Kings 22:6); in both instances the king receives an affirmative response. These parallels demonstrate that such requests for divine military direction were not unique to ancient Israel. At the same time, male and female "callers" delivered oracles from Ishtar of Arbela, including messages of salvation comparable to those in Second Isaiah, and these Assyrian oracles were preserved on clay tablets much like the words of the biblical prophets.

Upon the death of Esarhaddon in 669 B.C.E., his son Ashurbanipal assumed the Assyrian throne, and Shamash-shuma-ukin, another son, was installed as king of Babylon as a subordinate to Assyria. Ashurbanipal faced continued unrest in Egypt, leading to separate invasions in 667 and 663 B.C.E.; in the latter they not only recaptured Memphis but also extended Assyrian territorial control as far as Thebes. However, Ashurbanipal's attention was eventually required elsewhere, and Egypt was able to reassert its independence. The problem was Babylon. In 652 B.C.E. a civil war broke out between Ashurbanipal and his brother Shamash-shuma-ukin. The four-year-long struggle ended with the latter's defeat, at the cost of great hardship for the people of Babylon. This was then followed by Assyria's annihilation of Babylon's ally, Elam. In the meantime, Judah remained a loyal vassal under King Manasseh, such that Ashurbanipal's rule had little direct influence on the nation, other than its armies passing through on the way to Egypt.

Little is known about Ashurbanipal's final years, but in addition to the continued effort to hold the expanding Assyrian Empire together, the conflicts with Babylon and Elam in particular had two important consequences, namely, the weakening of Assyria due to the intense hostilities and the creation of a power vacuum to the east, one that was soon filled by the Medes and Persians. Upon Ashurbanipal's death in 627 B.C.E., his son Ashur-etil-ilani peacefully assumed the throne, but within three years he faced an internal rebellion by his general Sin-shumu-lishir, who deposed him in 620, only to be replaced in turn by Sin-shar-ishkun, Ashur-etil-ilani's brother, after another year of civil war. King Josiah took advantage of the situation to annex the Assyrian provinces of Samaria, Galilee, and Gilead. Meanwhile, the Assyrian king faced not only continued internal resistance but also outright rebellion by Babylonia, aided by the Medes (from what is western Iran today). The Medes conquered Ashshur in 614 B.C.E. and then aided the Chaldean Nabopolassar (625–605 B.C.E.) in overcoming the Assyrian capital Nineveh in 612 B.C.E., an event celebrated in the book of Nahum.

An Assyrian remnant held out for a few more years in Harran, supported by the Egyptians, who preferred a weak Assyria as a buffer between themselves and Babylonia.

In 609 B.C.E. Pharaoh Neco II set out with an army to aid the Assyrians and, along the way, killed King Josiah at Megiddo. The biblical text (2 Kings 23:29) says that "Josiah went to meet him" and that Neco killed him, but scholars dispute whether Josiah died in battle trying to stop Neco, perhaps thinking he would fare better with the Babylonians in power over all of Mesopotamia, or whether he simply went out to greet the pharaoh and was killed because Neco did not want to leave someone alive who could block his return after the battle. Either way, while the Egyptians failed to drive back the Babylonians and Medes, Judah came under Egyptian domination, with Josiah's son Jehoahaz being deposed and Jehoahaz's brother Jehoiakim installed as a puppet king.

Judah was now caught between Egypt and Babylonia, which fought each other for dominance. Once the Babylonians had defeated the Assyrians, they turned to deal with the Egyptians, driving them back at Carchemish in 605 B.C.E. The leader of the Babylonian army, Nebuchadnezzar, immediately returned to Babylon to assume the throne upon his father Nabopolassar's death but soon resumed his western campaigns, and Judah quickly submitted to Babylonia's authority. However, Neco inflicted a military defeat on the Babylonians in 601 B.C.E., causing Nebuchadnezzar to withdraw once again to Babylon, whereupon King Jehoiakim revolted against Babylonia. He then died (or was killed) in 598 B.C.E., and his son Jehoiachin surrendered to the Babylonian army in 597 B.C.E. Jehoiachin was replaced by his uncle Zedekiah, and Jehoiachin along with many leading citizens was deported to Babylonia. By 589 B.C.E., encouraged by "false prophets" who appealed to Isaiah's prophecies during Hezekiah's reign more than one hundred years earlier that Zion would not be overcome, and expecting Egyptian support, Zedekiah also rebelled. Nebuchadnezzar returned in force, but the Egyptians did not. This time Nebuchadnezzar ravaged the countryside and captured Jerusalem. King Zedekiah tried to escape during the night but was captured and brought before Nebuchadnezzar, who forced him to watch while his sons were killed, after which his eyes were put out (2 Kings 25:4-10). The Babylonians then leveled the city, destroyed the temple, and deported even more citizens.

This marked the beginning of the Babylonian Exile. This period is sometimes thought to have entailed the transfer of the entire population of Judah to Babylonia, leaving the land empty for decades, but the reality is that only a small portion of the population was taken, primarily from among the upper class. Babylonian records do not indicate how many were deported, but 2 Kings 24:14 says that 10,000 were removed in 598 B.C.E., although Jer 52:28 has a figure of only 3,023. More would have been taken after the final destruction of Jerusalem itself and again after the assassination of Gedaliah (see below). Thus Jer 52:30 states a total of 4,600 in three deportations. However, we must bear in mind that the number includes only men, and we must add in women and children, so the number in 2 Kings 24:14 may reflect the total number deported. If the population of Judah before the exile was in the vicinity of 250,000, this would constitute less than 5 percent of the total population.

What is certain is that the exiles were sufficiently numerous to form communities in Babylonia that eventually became self-sufficient and even prosperous. They were aided in this by the Babylonians' decision to settle them as groups (e.g., Ezek 1:1 mentions a group of exiles at the Chebar River), which helped them to preserve their ethnic and religious identity, although with effort. The presence of the exiled king Jehoiachin served as a symbol of unity as well, especially since a cuneiform tablet dated to the time of Nebuchadnezzar, about five years after Jerusalem's destruction, mentions rations being provided for Ya'ukina (=Jehoaichin), the king of Yahuda (=Judah) and his five sons, indicating they were given some measure of care and protection. Nevertheless, Psalm 137 expresses their sorrow and inability to "sing the LORD's song in a foreign land" (v. 4).

As for Judah, the majority of the population was probably left in the countryside; 2 Kings 24:14 states, "no one remained, except the poorest people of the land." Moreover, the Babylonians did not exchange population groups as the Assyrians did. As a result foreigners were not brought to Judah to replace those who had been taken. Therefore, those who remained in the land were neither displaced nor mixed together with people from elsewhere.

The Babylonians installed Gedaliah as governor at Mizpah, thirteen kilometers north of Jerusalem (2 Kings 25:22), with a garrison of Babylonian soldiers. Gedaliah headed a pro-Babylonian group and was a member of the family who had been friendly to Jeremiah (he was the son of Ahikam, son of Shaphan; cf. Jer 26:24), and he himself acted positively toward Jeremiah during his brief tenure as governor (Jer 40:11-12). Gedaliah did not serve long, however. At the instigation of King Baalis of Ammon, Ishmael, a Judean royal prince, killed Gedaliah and those with him (Jer 40:14; 2 Kings 25:25). Ishmael may have sought to reestablish a Judean kingdom, but other Judeans retaliated and Ishmael fled to Ammon. Those Judeans, fearing Babylonian retaliation, then fled to Egypt, forcing Jeremiah to go with them (Jeremiah 43). Little is known about the political rule in the land for the rest of the Babylonian period, although they undoubtedly installed another administrator. Nebuzaradan, the Babylonian commander who conquered Jerusalem in 586 B.C.E., established the poor remaining in the land as "vinedressers and tillers of the soil" (2 Kings 25:12) "and gave them vineyards and fields" (Jer 39:10). His goal appeared to be for the peasants to take over the estates of those deported, so that they might work them as a source of food and tribute for Babylon, and this would have continued after Gedaliah's death.

We can also reconstruct to some degree the state of the land and the situation of the population that remained. Most cities and towns were destroyed, although smaller unfortified villages survived. Archaeology confirms this; for example, Lachish, thirty-seven kilometers southwest of Jerusalem, was leveled and not resettled until about 450 B.C.E. Letters written on pieces of pottery and discovered in a guardhouse at Lachish indicate a breakdown in military discipline in the face of the Babylonian army, and one indicates that the signal fire from Azekah, nineteen kilometers away, had gone out, suggesting that it had already been overrun by the Babylonians. Jerusalem itself was also demolished, the Temple torn down, and the Babylonian soldiers permitted to loot the city. The Transjordanian states reclaimed their traditional territory and may have crossed the Jordan itself. Edom in particular occupied territory in southern Jordan, while Samaria moved its border south.

As for the people, many would have died in battle or been executed, while others would have succumbed to starvation and disease. Some fled to neighboring countries, but Jer 40:7-12 indicates some returned during Gedaliah's tenure. Still others went farther away: Jer 44:1 mentions Migdol, Tahpanhes, Memphis, and Upper Egypt (perhaps the military colony known to exist later at Elephantine). The result of all these factors combined was a drastic drop in the population, with some estimates indicating as few as twenty thousand people left in the land. In any case, the remaining people would not have been experienced statesmen and stateswomen, and so village and tribal customs reemerged after Gedaliah.

The general state of affairs and the people's reaction to it are described in Lamentations, which reads like an eyewitness account. Certainly, the Babylonian conquest created a pivotal theological challenge. The absence of a Davidic king on the throne implied that Yahweh had abandoned the covenant made with David (2 Samuel 7). More significantly, the destruction of the Temple, the Lord's house, ran counter to the belief in the permanence of Zion. Together these factors constituted a devastating blow to their religious beliefs, since it implied that Yahweh's power was less than that of Marduk, the Babylonians' national god. And if so, why not worship him instead or at least along with Yahweh? Thus, the Babylonian exile can truly be called a watershed event in the history of Israel. Seeing their country overrun, their capital devastated, their primary cultic site destroyed, and their leading citizens deported had a significant impact on the national psyche as well as posing a massive challenge to the religious traditions that up until then had given meaning to their lives. It would fall to the exilic prophets Jeremiah, Ezekiel, and Second Isaiah as well as to the compilers of the Deuteronomistic History and the priestly editors of the Pentateuch to explain these events and provide the theological insights that allowed the faith to continue.

After Nebuchadnezzar's death in 562 B.C.E., there were three Babylonian kings in six years. His son Amel-Marduk reigned for two years, but apart from the statement in 2 Kings 25:27-30 and Jer 52:31 that "Evil-merodach" released King Jehoiachin from prison, nothing is known of his reign. He was murdered by his brother-in-law Nergal-shar-usur (Nergal-sharezer in Jer 39:3); when Nergal-shar-usur died four years later, his own young son Labashi-Marduk was murdered after only nine months on the throne. Nabonidus (555–539 B.C.E.) served as the last ruler of the Neo-Babylonian Empire. He appears to have been an Assyrian and was dedicated to the moon god, Sin, promoting his worship in Ur over that of Marduk, the traditional chief of the Babylonian pantheon. This raised the opposition of the Marduk priests and was aggravated by his ten-year absence from the capital, Babylon, during which time he resided in Teima in Arabia, with his son Belshazzar serving as regent back in Babylonia.

Nabonidus is not mentioned in the First Testament, but his lengthy stay in Teima may be the basis for Nebuchadnezzar's seven-year madness (Dan 4:32), such that Nabonidus has been conflated with Nebuchadnezzar; this conflation is reinforced by the repeated references in Daniel 5 to Belshazzar as being Nebuchadnezzar's son. In any case, by the time Nabonidus returned to Babylonia in 543 B.C.E., the Persian ruler Cyrus had conquered Lydia and Media and was moving on Babylonia. In 539 B.C.E. Cyrus conquered the capital city, Babylon, and brought Nabonidus's reign to an end. Both Babylonian and Persian sources claim that the people opened the city gates and welcomed Cyrus as a liberator who restored the supremacy of Marduk's cult, although Herodotus claims there was a siege. In any case, the Persians now took over the Neo-Babylonian Empire and its territories, including Judah.

As mentioned earlier, by this time the Israelites would have likely been exposed to second-millennium Mesopotamian literature, such as Hammurabi's Code, *Enuma Elish, Atrahasis,* and *Gilgamesh,* during the Assyrian and then Babylonian domination of their homeland. At the same time, those deported by either empire would have experienced direct contact with the art and architecture of their conquerors. For example, they would have seen firsthand the hybrid deities called *keribu* that guarded Assyrian palaces and temples. Similarly, the Judahites deported to Babylon would have seen the high temple completed during the reign of Nebuchadnezzar. Only the foundations remain today of this ziggurat, a stepped pyramid, but they measure about three hundred square feet. The measurements given in a preserved tablet indicate its seven stories rose three hundred feet, and the shrine on top was called *Esagila* (the house that lifts up its head). This imposing structure undoubtedly influenced the story of the tower of Babel (the latter word is the Hebrew for Babylon) in Genesis 11, whose builders wanted to make its "top [literally "head"] in the heavens" (v. 4), only to have Yahweh undermine their efforts by introducing different languages and scattering them throughout the earth.

In addition, some points of contact between the Bible and the Mesopotamian literary remains from the First Millennium have already been mentioned in the course of the preceding historical survey, but a few more general ones deserve consideration. For instance, the general attitude of the Dialogue of Pessimism, from shortly after 1000 B.C.E., can be compared with the skeptical tone of Qoheleth. In the former a master proposes a series of opposing actions, and his servant always provides supporting arguments for each. For instance, in stanza 7, lines 46-52, we read:

Slave, listen to me! Here I am, master, here I am!
I want to make love to a woman! Make love, master, make love!
The man who makes love forgets sorrow and fear!
O well, slave, I do not want to make love to a woman.
Do not make love, master, do not make love.
Woman is a real pitfall, a hole, a ditch,
Woman is a sharp iron dagger that cuts a man's throat.

In addition to the similarity to the series of opposite actions in Qoh 3:1-9 (including "a time to embrace, and a time to refrain from embracing" in v. 5), this echoes Qoheleth's inability throughout his book to know with certainty what God requires of humanity.

There are also parallels between the poem of *Erra and Ishum* (Eighth Century B.C.E) and Ezekiel 21; 24–32, which have shared characteristics. Specifically, in both texts a god announces that he will kill both the just and the unjust in his rage, will destroy the entire country, will give the survivors to barbarians, will allow blood to flow through the city, will destroy trees, and will dry up rivers. Similarly, the "hand-raising" prayers (so called because they include liturgical directions to raise the hands in supplication at specific points) edited during the reign of Ashurbanipal share a common structure with the biblical Lament Psalms: there is an opening invocation of the deity, a description of the individual's situation and a petition for deliverance, and a concluding prayer of thanksgiving. Also, an Assyrian love song from this period describes the woman's thighs as gazelles, her ankles like apples, and her heels as obsidian, similar to descriptions in Song of Songs (7:1-5).

Two final points can be made with respect to developments in Israelite religion. First, the Queen of Heaven worshiped by Judahites (Jer 7:18; 44:17-19, 25) shows Assyrian influence: the word for the cakes that they make for her, *kawwānîm*, is derived from the Akkadian *kamānu*, which is used in Mesopotamian texts for offerings to Ishtar. However, the people's response (Jer 44:17) indicates that their devotion to the Queen of Heaven has been long-standing and therefore indigenous, so the best interpretation is that she is Astarte, albeit with some degree of syncretization with the Assyrian Ishtar. Second, some Mesopotamian texts have been proposed as the inspiration for, and even the source of, the assertions of monotheism found in Second Isaiah (Isa 40–55). Marduk is often said to be superior to all the other gods, much as Second Isaiah frequently asserts that Yahweh is incomparable, since there is no one else who can do the things Yahweh has done (e.g., Isa 40:18-20, 25-26; 41:1-4, 26-29; 44:6-7, etc.). One text even equates Marduk with the other gods, listing them in sequence and calling each Marduk of their respective primary function, as follows:

Sin,        Marduk who lights up the night

Shamash,   Marduk of justice

Adad,      Marduk of rain

and so on through the Babylonian pantheon. Another text identifies different deities with various aspects and attributes of Marduk, such as his kingship, his might, his wisdom, and so on, while still other texts identify the body parts of deities such as Marduk or Ishtar with the other gods, such that his or her face is one god, the eyes another, the mouth a third, and so on.

But although such texts may have been known to the prophet and may have influenced his movement to full monotheism, there are two important differences. One, as the last example shows, similar things are said about more than one god, with different devotees exalting different deities, which is the antithesis of true monotheism, understood as the belief in only one god. Two, Second Isaiah does not identify Yahweh with other gods like some of these texts do and earlier Israelites did with respect to Yahweh and El (see Chapter 6), nor does he attribute their characteristics to Yahweh, like in some of these other Mesopotamian texts and as Israelites did earlier with some of Baal's characteristics (also treated in Chapter 6). Instead, Second Isaiah flatly denies the existence of any other gods. Simply put, a statement such as, "There is no other god besides me. . . . I am God, and there is no other" (Isa 45:21-22), goes far beyond the claims made about Marduk or Ishtar. Second Isaiah does not just assert Yahweh's superiority to or embodiment of other deities; he asserts Yahweh's uniqueness and exclusivity!

CHAPTER 2

# Egypt

The history of ancient Egypt under the pharaohs is traditionally organized in terms of thirty dynasties, a system introduced in the Third Century B.C.E. by an Egyptian priest
named Manetho and still used today. The First Dynasty is associated with King Meni, who is said to have united Upper and
Lower Egypt around 3100 B.C.E., and the Thirtieth Dynasty ends in
342 B.C.E. with the defeat of Nectanebo II and the restoration of
direct Persian rule. Since the first fourteen dynasties, extending up
to the Seventeenth Century B.C.E., predate the rise of biblical Israel
by four centuries and have no major relevance for understanding
Israel's history, I will not discuss them here, although I will later
examine some literature from this period.

## The Second Intermediate Period
## (ca. 1650–1550 B.C.E.)

Instead, I start with the latter part of the Second Intermediate
Period, during which Egypt was dominated by a series of foreign
rulers the Egyptians called the *Hyksos*, meaning "rulers of foreign
lands." They were a Semitic people, part of the Amorites who had
also spread into Mesopotamia during the Second Millennium
B.C.E. Although a significant number of Semitic people had been

31

infiltrating the eastern delta region for years, the evidence supports Manetho's claim that the Hyksos period was initiated by a sudden invasion. The Hyksos established control of the region ca. 1648 B.C.E., with their capital at Avaris, and their sphere of influence soon spread through the rest of Upper Egypt, with other Egyptian dynasties serving as their vassals. After about a century, organized resistance began with Seqenenre Tao II of the Seventeenth Dynasty in Thebes. When his son Kamose came to the throne, he led an army northward and, after a series of successful battles, laid siege to Avaris but was not able to overcome it. It fell to his brother Ahmose, the founder of the Eighteenth Dynasty, to complete the task and drive the Hyksos out of Egypt, pursuing them into Palestine.

The Hyksos have been linked to the First Testament in two ways. The first is as the context for the Joseph story. A period in which Semitic rulers held sway over Egypt is an appropriate narrative context for Joseph, a Semite, to rise to the position of the pharaoh's second in command, since in general the Hyksos would be more receptive to the subsequent immigration of his extended family. However, in the absence of any extrabiblical record of either event, all we can say is that it presents a plausible setting for the Joseph story but cannot be used to demonstrate its historical accuracy. The other suggested connection with the First Testament is that the expulsion of the Hyksos is the basis for the Exodus tradition. This is unlikely on two grounds, however. The first is that the Hyksos were driven out of Egypt three centuries before the likely date of the Exodus, and the second is that the Israelites were unlikely under any circumstance to invent the idea that they had been slaves in Egypt, but especially if they or their ancestors had been its rulers. Thus, the Hyksos period remains an intriguing period of Egyptian history but unfortunately one with little relevance to a better understanding of the biblical traditions.

## The New Kingdom (ca. 1550–1069 B.C.E.)

Although Ahmose followed the fleeing Hyksos into Palestine, destroying them there, he did not exploit that incursion, opting instead to conquer the Hyksos's allies to the south, the Nubians.

Thus, the first three kings of the Eighteenth Dynasty adopted a primarily defensive posture with respect to its northern borders, punctuated with occasional raids to seize some of their neighbors' resources; one of these under Thutmose I reached as far as the Euphrates but did not result in any permanent military presence in Syro-Palestine, without which he could not command the allegiance of its rulers. However, when the ruler of Qadesh on the Orontes River formed an alliance about twenty years later with some three hundred city-states and gathered an army from among them at Megiddo, the Egyptians feared a repeat of the Hyksos invasion and preempted any possibility of this with an attack of their own. In 1482 B.C.E., Thutmose III conducted a seven-month siege of Megiddo that resulted in oaths of loyalty from the princes involved.

Although this confirmed Egyptian control of Palestine, conflicts continued with smaller nations to the north that were vassals of Mitanni, the Hurrian kingdom spanning Mesopotamia, northern Syria, and southeast Anatolia (see further in Chapter 6), and this eventually resulted in direct conflict between the two major powers. The rest of the Fifteenth Century B.C.E. saw repeated attacks and counterattacks between Egypt and Mitanni until, facing additional pressure from the encroaching Hittites to the northwest, Mitanni cemented a peace with Egypt through the marriage of the king's daughter to Thutmose IV ca. 1415 B.C.E. Syro-Palestine was divided between the two nations, with Egyptian control extending along the Mediterranean coast into what is now Lebanon and inland to Qadesh, which had become an Egyptian vassal.

Although there were occasional localized rebellions that were easily put down, Egypt's territorial control over these lands was largely unchallenged for the next sixty-five years and was accompanied by internal prosperity and harmony. The internal situation changed, however, with the ascension of Amenhotep IV (1350–1334 B.C.E.) to the throne. He immediately promoted the worship of the sun disk, the Aten, over that of the traditional chief deity in Egypt, Amun-Re. Then in his fifth year, he changed his name to Akhenaten ("One who is effective on behalf of the Aten") and built a new capital at the site of the modern Tell el-Amarna, which he named Akhetaten ("the Horizon of the Sun Disk"). Not long afterward, he closed the temples to other gods and suppressed their cult. His religious policies did not long survive his death, however. After a brief reign by his son Smenkhkare, Akhenaten's other son Tutankhaten came to the throne at the age of nine or ten, and three years into his reign the latter ended the cult of the Aten, restored the worship of Amun-Re to prominence, changed his own name to Tutankhamun, and moved the capital back to Thebes. In subsequent years, great effort was made to destroy any record of Akhenaten, including erasing his name from monuments and destroying visual representations of the dead ruler.

Much has been made of Akhenaten's supposed monotheism, with some suggesting it was the basis for Moses' beliefs. Without entering into the debate as to whether Moses and his followers were true monotheists, the span of one hundred years between Akhenaten and Moses, coupled with the concerted effort to remove Akhenaten from history by the priests of Amun-Re, make it highly unlikely that anyone was even aware of Akhenaten and his beliefs by the time Moses came on the scene. Moreover, Akhenaten's short-lived religious reform was not itself monotheistic. Although the royal family worshiped the Aten, Egyptians were expected to worship Akhenaten. This is just one of many differences between Akhenaten's religion and that of the Israelites, namely, for the latter Yahweh entered into a relationship with the entire people rather than just a single individual. Moreover, the Aten cult contains none of the ritual components or the emphasis on justice found in Yahwism. Also, Yahweh was understood primarily as a storm god or a warrior god rather than a solar deity. Thus, those trying to identify the basis for Israelite monotheism have to look elsewhere.

A slightly more qualified conclusion can be reached for the relationship between the Great Hymn to the Aten, found in a tomb at el-Amarna, and Psalm 104. There are a number of common points in the two works, as the following chart demonstrates:

| Great Hymn to the Aten (by lines) | Psalm 104 (by verses) |
| --- | --- |
| 11-12: when the Aten sets it is dark | 20: Yahweh makes the night dark |
| 17: lions prowl at night | 21: young lions hunt at night |

| 21-24: the rising Aten dispels the darkness | 22: lions withdraw when the sun rises |
|---|---|
| 30: the whole land works during the day | 23: people work until sunset |
| 31-34: cattle graze, plants grow, birds nest | 11: animals drink<br>12: birds nest<br>14: plants grow |
| 37, 39: ships sail on and fish swim in the water | 25-26: ships sail on the sea, which is full of fish, including Leviathan |
| 52: "How manifold are your works" | 24: "How manifold are your works" |
| 54: the Aten alone created the world | 24: Yahweh has made every-thing |
| 60: the Aten provides food | 27: people look to Yahweh for food |
| 70-73: rain makes waves on the mountains that in turn water fields | 10: water flows between the hills<br>13: the heavens water the mountains |
| 99-100: people live when the Aten rises and die when it sets | 29-30: Yahweh's presence is positive and his absence is negative |

But despite these sometimes striking similarities, there are also important differences. First, the similarities appear in a different order in each poem. Second, night has negative connotations in the Aten hymn that are lacking in the psalm. Third, the sun is the cause of creation in the hymn but the object of creation in Psalm 104. Fourth, the psalm is not Nile centered and does not include the hymn's attention to human embryos and unhatched chicks. Psalm 104 displays equally significant parallels with Genesis 1 but with a much closer agreement in terms of the sequence of material.

As such, the affinities between the Great Hymn to the Aten and Psalm 104 are perhaps best attributed to their shared subject matter, namely, the relationship of a deity to creation.

A more profitable point of discussion in relationship to Akhenaten is the collection of tablets written in Akkadian, the language of international communication at the time, found at el-Amarna, the site of his capital and dating to his reign. Among these are letters to the major powers in Mesopotamia, Mitanni, and Hatti with which Egypt interacted on the international stage, as well as even more numerous letters to and from Egyptian vassals in Canaan and Syria. The latter provide a glimpse into the disinterested nature of Egyptian rule in the area during this period. A number of the vassals complain about the lack of military protection, citing the withdrawal of Egyptian soldiers and archers. They also reflect great rivalry among the city-states of Syro-Palestine, with reports of attacks by one on another and accusations of treason against Egypt itself.

Connected to this are the frequent references to *ʿapiru* (sometimes written as *ḫabiru*). The term, which is applied to both individuals and groups, is a social designation for people living outside the boundaries of mainstream society. The *ʿapiru* sometimes appear in the Amarna texts as roving bands of outlaws and at other times as mercenaries, hired servants, day laborers, and holders of other marginal social roles. The term was generally used derogatorily and was not restricted to the lower class. For example, Rib-Adda of Byblos calls ʿAbdi-Ashirta of Amurru and his son ʿAziru *ʿapiru*, with the implication that they have rebelled against Pharaoh. Due to the similarity in spelling between *ʿapiru* and Hebrew (especially when the former is written as *ḫabiru*), when these tablets were first discovered, some scholars saw confirmation of the Israelite invasion of Canaan as narrated in the book of Joshua. However, apart from yet another time gap, the *ʿapiru* of the Amarna documents are in no way as organized or as numerous as the Israelites led by Joshua, as seen from the fact that ʿAbdi-Heba of Jerusalem asks for a mere fifty men to guard his city against his attackers. Nonetheless, the Amarna texts are relevant to the issue of early Israel in that the same lack of Canaanite political unity accompanied by social unrest also prevailed in the area during the Israelites' early years in Canaan.

After Tutankhamun's death without an heir at the age of nine-teen or twenty (ca. 1325 B.C.E.), his vizier, Ay, ruled for four years and, after his death, was followed by the Egyptian general Horemheb. Horemheb also was childless, so he appointed another military commander as Ramesses I, the founder of the Nineteenth Dynasty. He died within two years and was followed by his son, Seti I (ca. 1291–1279 B.C.E.), who is often considered to be the pharaoh who enslaved the Israelites. Seti I reasserted Egyptian power in the north, taking back the city of Qadesh on the Orontes River and the Amurru region south of there from the Hittites (see Chapter 3). When the Hittites under the rule of King Muwatalli II once again conquered Qadesh, Ramesses II, who had succeeded his father, Seti, led an army of four divisions north. The two forces met at Qadesh. The Hittites ambushed the Egyptians, who had been deceived by Hittite spies posing as deserters and claiming that the Hittite army was still at Aleppo, two hundred kilometers to the north. Ramesses managed to rally his troops, yet despite his claims of victory, the battle ended in a stalemate. The result was that Hatti reclaimed Amurru as well, and the border between the two powers returned to where it had been before. After this, rela-tions between the two empires improved to the point that a treaty was formalized in 1259 B.C.E. The mutual support this embodied was solidified by the marriage of a Hittite princess to Ramesses in 1246 B.C.E. The result was that Egypt's control of Canaan was once again secure, and there is no record of any additional military incursions for many years.

Ramesses II has been proposed as the Pharaoh of the Exodus on a number of grounds. First, his reign coincides with the usual date for the Exodus in the middle of the Thirteenth Century. Second, Exod 1:11 refers to the enslaved Israelites building the cities of Pithom and Ramesses. If the latter is correctly identified with Piramesses, Ramesses' new capital at modern-day Khatana-Qantir in the northeast Nile delta, which is coincidentally a convenient starting point for the departing Israelites, the connection would be relatively secure. It would be even stronger if the site of Pithom was known, but unfortunately, there is no consensus on that point. Nevertheless, the association of Ramesses with any exodus is supported by the third point, namely, that his successor Merneptah referred early in his reign to "Israel," a rural people in the central highlands of Israel, which means they would need to have left Egypt during Ramesses' reign in order to make the journey and settle in the highlands.

Ramesses II was followed by his son Merneptah (ca. 1212–1202 B.C.E.), who also figures in reconstructing the early history of Israel. In his fifth year he turned back attacks by the combined forces of Libyans and the Sea Peoples (for the latter see further in Chapter 6), which is commemorated in the Merneptah Stele, an inscribed memorial pillar dated to ca. 1207 B.C.E. More significant for our purposes is a reference to "Israel" in this inscription. The relevant section reads:

> Plundered is the Canaan with every evil;
> Carried off is Ashkelon; seized upon is Gezer
> Yanoam is made as that which does not exist;
> Israel is laid to waste, his seed is not;
> Hurru has become a widow for Egypt!

This text is significant simply by virtue of being the earliest known extrabiblical reference to Israel, but it also provides further insights into the origins of ancient Israel. *Canaan* and *Hurru* are synonymous terms, indicating that what is mentioned between them falls within the same region. Ashkelon is in the coastal plain, Gezer is located in the lowlands, and Yanoam is even farther inland. If we follow this trajectory, Israel would be located in the central highlands, precisely where a large number of new settlements emerged at the end of the Thirteenth Century B.C.E. Moreover, each of the names is preceded by a sign known as a determinative, meant to indicate the class of noun that follows. Ashkelon, Gezer, and Yanoam are preceded by the sign for a city, whereas Israel has the determinative for a rural group of people. In other words, the Egyptians viewed Israel as an established entity, although one that had yet to settle into cities.

Related to this are pictures at the temple of Karnak that also derive from Merneptah. Among the various pictorial panels is one that is labeled "Ashkelon" and depicts a city being attacked and ultimately defeated by Egyptian forces. Adjacent to this panel are three others, two of which also depict a city being attacked while the third shows a battle in open country. The explicit identification of the first one as Ashkelon, one of the cities named in

Merneptah's stele, supports identifying the other three panels with the other two cities plus an unsettled population mentioned in the stele. However, in all four panels the defenders are represented with the same hairstyle and attire. Since the Egyptians were careful to distinguish among various nations in their graphic art, this indicates that they did not recognize any distinction between Canaanites and Israelites. This, in turn, is relevant for any discussion of the origins of ancient Israel, especially for theories that consider a significant portion of early Israel to be Canaanites.

Egyptian control of Canaan effectively ended during the reign of Ramesses III, at the beginning of the Twelfth Century B.C.E. A major factor was his battles with the Sea Peoples, large groups of people migrating from the Aegean, who were already responsible for the collapse of the Hittite Empire, Ugarit, and smaller nation states along the Mediterranean coast (see further in Chapters 1 and 6). Ramesses managed to repel these invaders in a series of land and sea battles, but the effort left Egypt significantly weakened and unable to protect its vassals in Canaan. One group of Sea Peoples, the Peleset, settled along the coast of Israel and become known as the biblical Philistines.

Internal political and economic problems further weakened Egypt's position both at home and abroad. The reduction of Egypt's international influence is reflected in the story of Wen-amun, a messenger sent to Byblos near the end of Ramesses XI's reign (ca. 1080–1070 B.C.E.) to obtain a supply of lumber. Despite his official mission, he was robbed along the way and treated rudely by Zerkarbaal, the king of Byblos, who ordered him to leave with the retort, "I am not the servant of the one who sent you." This episode is a far cry from that of earlier days when Egyptian officials were feared and honored. Wen-amun was successful only after his god, Amun, took possession of a court seer and ordered the king to receive Wen-amun. This ecstatic prophet parallels both Israelite and non-Israelite ecstatics in the biblical literature, including Balaam (Num 24:3-4, 15-16), Baʿal's prophets (1 Kings 18:21), Saul and two groups of ecstatic prophets, the second of which was led by Samuel (1 Sam 10:5-13; 19:18-24), Elisha (2 Kings 3:15), and perhaps Jeremiah (cf. Jer 20:9; 23:9). In short, this phenomenon was not unique to biblical Israel, and as we will see in Chapter 6, it was found elsewhere as well.

# The Third Intermediate Period (ca. 1069–664 B.C.E.)

Egypt's weakness at this time allowed for the establishment of Israel as an independent nation, after which Egypt managed only occasional forays into the region. Sheshonq I invaded in "the fifth year of King Rehoboam" (1 Kings 14:25; ca. 917 B.C.E.); the initial biblical account, where he is called Shishak, says only that Rehoboam gave him the entire royal and temple treasuries (1 Kings 14:26), but the parallel in 2 Chron 12:1-12 provides much more detail, including that this was punishment for turning away from God. Sheshonq's version in the temple of Amun at Karnak lists some 150 places that he claims to have conquered. Jerusalem is not mentioned, supporting the biblical version, but a number of cities in the north are, despite the fact that Sheshonq had earlier sheltered King Jeroboam from Solomon (1 Kings 11:40). Archaeological evidence indicates destruction levels at many of the sites named by Sheshonq, but Sheshonq was unable to retain a military presence in the region, and his invasion really constituted an extended raid. After this, the growing power of Assyria and then Babylon kept Egypt out of Israel's affairs for the most part. The report of Asa's rout of a massive force led by the otherwise unknown "Zerah the Ethiopian" (2 Chron 14:8-14) is fictional and clearly aims to emphasize the divine intervention involved, while Hoshea's attempt to form an alliance with the equally unattested "King So of Egypt" (2 Kings 17:4) is said to have failed anyway. The few other instances of Egyptian interaction with Israel are treated in greater detail elsewhere in this book: Egypt's involvement with Hezekiah's rebellion against Sennacherib and Pharaoh Neco's role in the death of Josiah are treated in Chapter 1, as are the Assyrian and Babylonian invasions of Egypt. Egypt's subjection to Persia and Greece will be discussed in Chapters 4 and 5, respectively.

# Additional Egyptian Literature

A significant portion of ancient Egyptian literature is illustrative for the biblical literature in terms of both the mode of expression and the thematic content. The prime example of the former is the Egyptian Instruction genre, which is structured in three parts:

1.  A direct address to "my son," reflecting the scribal tradition for a student and containing a command that he "hear," "listen," and so on.
2.  The motive for listening and obeying. The reasons are usually the benefits that derive from the teaching. There is little appeal to anything beyond the presumably self-evident value of the teaching itself. The only authority referred to is the teacher, indicated by "my son," "my instruction," and so on.
3.  The teaching itself. The focus is on exhortation and argumentation in support of the teaching, distinguishing it from the tendency in shorter wisdom sayings to make an observation and leave the moral up to the reader or listener.

This structure is clearly seen in Prov 1:8-19:

1. A call to hear:   "Hear, my child, your father's instruction" (v. 8).
2. The motive:       it will be like flowers and jewelry (v. 9).
3. The teaching:     avoid robbers (vv. 10-19).

It is also present in Prov 2:1-22:

1. A call to hear:   Verse 1 urges the child to "accept" and "treasure" his words, and verses 2-4 introduce wisdom as the object of the reader's desire, with verbs such as be "attentive," "incline (your heart)," "seek," and "search" while asking for "insight" and "understanding."
2. The motive:       This will result in religious understanding (vv. 5-8), which leads to ethical understanding (vv. 9-11) that will deliver the reader from both evil men (vv. 12-15) and adulterous women (vv. 16-19).
3. The teaching:     There are two "paths," that of the good and that of the wicked, a common theme in the Wisdom literature (vv. 20-22).

Once aware of this structure, the reader can recognize it eight more times in the opening chapters of Proverbs, with each reflecting the content of Proverbs 2. Proverbs 3:1-12 deals with a proper relationship with God, 3:21-35 discusses the two ways, 4:1-9 is concerned with the value of wisdom, 4:10-19 urges that one avoid the actions of the wicked, 4:20-27 deals with avoiding perverse speech, and 5:1-23; 6:20-35, and 7:1-27 discuss the adulterous woman.

Examples of the Egyptian Instruction genre span some two thousand years, covering topics that are frequently addressed in Israelite Wisdom literature as well. The focus is usually on how one should function at and within the royal court, and this motif is often assisted by attributing the instruction to one of the pharaohs or else to one of their advisors. But even when such an explicit connection is not made, the purpose remains the same, as can be seen by the nature of the advice. Emphasis is given to topics such as how to deal with one's inferiors and superiors, proper table manners, the importance of truthfulness and courtesy, and warnings about and against women. Within the setting of the royal household, all such suggestions served a practical purpose in ensuring that one did not offend the king in one's words or actions. The ideals that were held forth for imitation reflected the societal norms of proper behavior as well as its biases and prejudices. Symptomatic of this is the negative view of women. Since scribes were male, the instructions tend to paint women as temptresses who would seek to seduce the young pupil and lead him astray. The dangers involved when such women were part of the royal harem or related to influential members of the court would seem obvious to all, and thus they were consistently warned against becoming involved with them, however innocently that relationship might begin.

The oldest Egyptian instructions we have come from the period of the Old Kingdom, with the most important one being that of *Ptahhotep* (ca. 2450 B.C.E.). This work is indicative of the content I have just outlined: the emphasis is on caution in one's speech and actions. Ptahhotep stresses the importance of knowing one's place at all times and in all things, and he is especially insistent about the erotic dangers of women at the court: "One is made a fool by limbs of fayence, as she stands there, become all carnelian. A mere trifle, the likeness of a dream—and one attains death by knowing her." The lures of the adulterous woman are described similarly in

Prov 5:3-6; 6:24-25; 7:13, 16-17, and the same deadly fate awaits those she seduces, while Qoh 7:26-28 expresses an even more negative view of women. Ptahhotep concludes his work by discussing the two possible responses to his advice, urging that it be heard and obeyed as the means to prosperity and success rather than be rejected.

Two other instructions from this period are in a fragmentary state. Only the ending has survived from the *Instruction of Kagemni,* and that section deals with table manners and the value of wise speech. Just a few lines survive from *Prince Hardjedef,* warning against boasting and advising marriage, but the frequent references to him in later literature suggest that he is to be associated with a more extensive and significant tradition.

The instructions of *King Merikare* and *King Amenemhet* are representative of works from the Second Kingdom period. Both contain an element of pessimism in light of the political upheaval that Egypt had experienced. In addition to the traditional concerns, Merikare focuses on defense of the state and introduces final judgment as a motivation for wise behavior. Amenemhet was killed ca. 1950 B.C.E. as the result of a plot from within his harem. The posthumous nature of his address indicates that we are dealing with a literary creation, but his advice to his son centers on the fact that the son cannot trust anyone since his father was assassinated by those he trusted.

After the Hyksos rulers (ca. 1650–1550 B.C.E.), we find a greater stress on individual piety. The older view that the divine order was reflected in the political state had been shattered, and scribes sought to contact God not through Pharaoh as the embodiment of the divine but through prayer and worship. Ethical considerations and love of God become motivating factors for proper behavior, and an air of passivity can be detected. Into this time frame fall *Ani* and *Amenemope,* both of which share the characteristics I have outlined. The latter is especially important because of its parallels with Prov 22:17–24:22, in terms of both structure and content. *Amenemope* consists of thirty chapters while Prov 22:20 refers to "thirty sayings." Moreover, there is a high degree of verbal identity between the opening of this section of Proverbs and the beginning of the instruction proper in *Amenemope* (after the introduction); the following chart presents identical and nearly identical terms in bold and comparable words with underlining:

| Proverbs 22:17-18 | *Amenemope* 3:9-11, 13, 16 |
|---|---|
| The words of the wise: Incline **your ear** and **hear** my **words,** and apply **your mind** to <u>my teaching</u>; for **it will be pleasant** if you<br><br>**keep them within you,**<br><br>if all of them are ready on **your lips**. | Give **your ears** and **hear what is said**<br>Give **your mind** over to <u>their interpretation</u><br>**It is profitable** to **put them** in your heart<br>**Let them rest** in the shrine of **your insides**<br>They will be a mooring post on **your tongue** |

The following verses in Proverbs contain a large number of additional parallels that go beyond a simple similarity of content or theme to encompass similar wording. Once again, the following chart represents some of the correspondence between the two works:

| Proverbs | *Amenemope* |
|---|---|
| "Do not **rob** <u>the poor</u> because they are poor" (22:22). | "Guard against **robbing** <u>the oppressed</u>" (4:4; chap. 2). |
| "<u>Make no friends with those given to anger</u>" (22:24). | "<u>Do not associate with a heated man</u>" (11:13; chap. 9). |
| "Do you see those who are <u>skillful in their work</u>?" (22:29). | "As for the scribe who is <u>experienced in his office</u>" (27:16; chap. 30). |
| "When you sit down to **eat** with a **ruler**" (23:1). | "Do not **eat** bread before a **noble**" (23:13; chap. 23). |

| "<u>Do not wear yourself out to get rich</u>" (23:4). | "<u>Do not strain to seek an excess</u>" (9:14: chap. 7). |
|---|---|
| "**Do not remove** an ancient **landmark**" (23:10). | "**Do not carry** off the **land-mark** at the boundaries" (7:12; chap. 6). |

These comparisons point to a definite literary relationship, indicating that one has relied on the other, and the evidence supports Proverbs' dependence on *Amenemope*. One factor is adaptation to an Israelite context. For instance, Prov 22:22 adds a reference to "the gate" as the location for the administration of justice, a common motif in the First Testament, and the landmark in *Amenemope* simply marks arable land while in Proverbs it is linked with injustice to orphans, yet another biblical theme. Conversely, some words and phrases in Prov 22:17 are found only there in the First Testament, suggesting they have been borrowed. Inclining one's ear to hear is a common metaphor, but it is never combined with "mind," while "within you" is literally "in your belly" rather than the usual "in your kidneys." The parallels end at Prov 23:11, which could be explained as the author working from his memory of *Amenemope*, and even though he could not remember the rest of his source text, he still employed the organizational feature of the number thirty while incorporating his own material in the second part of the section.

The *Instruction of Onkhsheshonqy* was written in demotic, a late form of the Egyptian language, in the Fifth Century B.C.E. The author was implicated in a palace coup and wrote his advice to his son on broken pieces of pottery while imprisoned. This work is marked by the extensive use of proverbial material, often of one line, rather than the more developed address of earlier instructions. It is significant that although it is addressed to his son, it appears to be directed to the general populace by virtue of its more generalized content. A similar use of the proverbial form can be seen in *Papyrus Insinger*, from the Fourth/Third Century B.C.E., which replaces the ideal of silence with that of balance and insists that god will punish those who upset the equilibrium. Such collections of proverbs are paralleled in the books of

Proverbs and the deuterocanonical Sirach, and to a lesser extent, Qoheleth.

The conservative strain of Egyptian wisdom is also contained in works that support and praise the scribal tradition. Onomastica may fall into this category, inasmuch as they seek to present the current state of scribal knowledge of the world. Lists of things arranged in various categories of similarity or contrast were periodically updated as further divisions became recognized. By comparing the chronological development among these noun lists, we can trace the expansion of the scribes' knowledge and the ongoing attempts to categorize, order, and structure their experience of the world around them. A similar desire to relate different aspects of human experience is found in number sayings of Prov 30:15-16, 18-19, 21-28, 29-31.

Egyptian works from various periods expand at greater length than *Amenemope* on the value of the scribal tradition, comparing it with the labor and drudgery of other professions. In the *Instruction of Khety* (ca. 1750 B.C.E.), only the scribal profession is a pleasant one, and it is valued even beyond love of one's mother. *In Praise of Learned Scribes* (ca. 1300 B.C.E.) argues that scribes gained greater immortality through their wisdom being cited than others did through pyramids or inscriptions. *The Instruction of a Man for His Son* stresses the power of a teacher-scribe to impart knowledge while *Papyrii Sallier* and *Anastasi* contrast the scribal profession to the treatment given to a field hand and a soldier, respectively. In the same way, Sir 38:24–39:11 reviews the work of farmers, artisans, smiths, and potters but finds them all inferior to the scribe.

A more skeptical strain in Egyptian wisdom is reflected in what can be categorized as discussion literature, in which the traditional views about reality and society are called into question. In the fables and debates this is raised but not carried to extremes; however, a number of works challenge the traditional foundations of Egyptian society, much like the books of Job and Qoheleth. The *Tale of the Eloquent Peasant* has structural and thematic similarities to Job. Like Job, it consists of prose sections surrounding nine semipoetic speeches. A peasant whose property has been stolen repeatedly challenges the injustice of his situation, becoming more eloquent with each speech until his property (and more) is restored to him. However, unlike Job, his situation is caused by one human, and he makes his eloquent appeals to other humans, whereas Job is afflicted by God and demands a hearing before the deity. Qoheleth displays a similar skepticism concerning order in the world, the abuse of power, and the ability to determine what is right, as well as a sense of weariness with the accumulated wisdom like that found in *Lamentations of Khakheperre-sonbe. The Dispute over Suicide* (also known as the *Dialogue of a Man with His Soul*) goes further and despairs over ever finding any justice at all. Once again we have a poetic discussion surrounded by prose in which an individual espouses the value of suicide in the face of injustice, since his suffering will end and his situation will be different in the afterlife; neither suicide nor an afterlife are concepts found in Job. In response, the soul argues that the role of humans on earth is to enjoy whatever pleasures can be found in this life. The latter theme is echoed in the *Song of the Harper* and recurs a number of times in Qoheleth (see 2:24; 3:12-13, 22; 5:17-18; 8:15; cf. 11:9). Finally, a number of other works criticize the lack of order in Egypt and long for an individual who can dispel the apparent chaos.

A final point of comparison with the book of Job comes from the declarations of innocence in the Egyptian Book of the Dead. These fill at least 192 chapters of differing length with assertions of things that an individual has not done, with the goal of asserting one's moral character during the divine judgment of the dead. Similarly, Job 31 contains Job's oath of innocence prior to the hearing he anticipates having before God, in which he, too, lists a number of things that he has not done, although he formulates his oath as a series of conditional statements followed by negative consequences that should befall him if he has actually done the first thing ("if I have . . . then let"). There is even some degree of overlap between the Book of the Dead and Job in terms of the offenses both deny committing, such as succumbing to adultery (Job 31:9), being unjust to slaves (Job 31:13), denying food to children (Job 31:16), acting against orphans (Job 31:18, 21), and being greedy (Job 31:24-25), thereby indicating a common human understanding of basic right and wrong.

Other types of Egyptian literature illuminate the biblical literature as well. Two narratives exhibit plot elements similar to some biblical narratives. The first is the story of Sinuhe, purported to be an official under Pharaoh Amenemhet I, who reigned at the beginning of the Second Millennium. When Amenemhet dies, Sinuhe overhears a conversation indicating that the pharaoh had been assassinated, so he flees to Syro-Palestine, protected by the goddess Hathor, in order to avoid being killed by the traitors. He lives there among some herders and marries their leader's daughter. When he is challenged to a duel by a "strong man" armed with a shield, an ax, and javelins, he defeats him with a single arrow and then cuts off his head. Many years later, after learning that the rightful heir sits on the throne, he returns in triumph to Egypt. This tale has similarities to the life of Moses, who also flees Egypt to escape being killed, marries the daughter of herders with whom he lives, and eventually returns to Egypt in triumph. At the same time, there is some parallel to Joseph, who is protected by God, is taken to Egypt, rises to a position of importance, and is eventually reunited with his family. In addition, the episode of Sinuhe's one-on-one combat is frequently compared with David's victory over Goliath. Nevertheless, despite these similarities, the differences in each case undercut the possibility of direct influence on the biblical stories, but they reflect shared narrative developments.

A second Egyptian story that is often related to the Joseph story is the Tale of Two Brothers. Bata lives with his older brother, Anubis, and they work together on Anubis's farm, growing crops and raising cattle. One day when Bata returns home in the middle of the day to get additional seed for planting, Anubis's wife propositions him, but he rejects her advances and returns to the fields. She drinks grease to induce vomiting and dishevels herself, and when Anubis returns at the end of the day, she claims that Bata tried to seduce her and beat her when she refused. Bata is forced to flee for his life, is protected by one of the gods, vows his innocence to his brother, and cuts off his penis to show his sincerity. He then flees into Syro-Palestine while Anubis goes home and kills his wife. After various other events, the two brothers are reconciled, and Bata becomes pharaoh, followed by Anubis. As has long been recognized, the basic plot line also appears in Gen 39:7-20. The wife of Potiphar, Joseph's master, repeatedly attempts to seduce Joseph and then, threatened with exposure, claims that

Joseph tried to assault her sexually, with the result that Joseph is put in prison.

A final type of literature to consider is Egyptian love songs found in storage rooms used by Ramesses II. They share with the biblical Song of Songs an unabashed celebration of the emotional and physical joys of love between a man and a woman. More particularly, both include descriptions of a lover's body using metaphors that sound strange to modern ears. For instance, in one Egyptian song, the male describes his lover's body as follows:

> Her lips are a lotus bud
> Her breasts are mandrake blossoms
> Her arms are vines
> Her eyes are berries
> Her head is a snare of willows
> And I am the goose. (#3, 309)

This song can be compared with the descriptions of the woman in the Song of Songs that describe her hair as goats, her teeth as ewes, her neck and her nose as towers, and so on, as well as descriptions of the male using comparable metaphors from nature (see Song 4:1-6; 5:10-15; 6:4-7; 7:1-9). Reading the Egyptian and Israelite poems together reminds us that our modern notions of what constitutes flattery were not necessarily shared by our ancient predecessors.

CHAPTER 3

# Hatti

The Hittites were an Indo-European people who flourished in central Anatolia (modern-day Turkey) during the Second Millennium B.C.E. After their empire collapsed (ca. 1180 B.C.E.), various Neo-Hittite states emerged in central Anatolia and northern Syria. The term *Hittite* is based on an identification of this group with the Hittites mentioned in the Bible. They themselves referred to their land as Hatti, which comes from the indigenous population of the territory prior to the emergence of the Hittites.

## History

The Hittites established a kingdom with their capital at Hattusa (modern-day Bogazköy, about 150 kilometers east of Ankara) in 1690 B.C.E. and quickly expanded their power over the surrounding territory. Before long they began to exert control of the trade routes through northern Syria, in the process making the regional powers and city-states their vassals. At the beginning of the Sixteenth Century B.C.E. the Hittites sacked Babylon, effectively ending the dynasty established two centuries before by Hammurabi, although they did not annex the land itself. Despite these successes, however, the Hittites still had to deal with periodic unrest within their territory and attack from without.

The reign of Tudhaliya II, beginning circa 1400 B.C.E., marked the transition from a kingdom toward an empire. Tudhaliya put down a series of regional uprisings, entered into treaties with others, and solidified Hittite power in Syria. Yet less than fifty years later the surrounding nations combined their forces to attack Hatti and burn the capital of Hattusa. The royal family escaped, however, and Tudhaliya III set about recapturing Anatolia, a process that took a few decades. During this period, Queen Ankhesenamun, the widow of Tutankhamun, sent an envoy asking King Suppiluliuma to provide one of his sons to replace her dead husband. Suspicious of the request, the Hittite king sent his own envoy to Egypt to confirm the situation, prompting an irritated response from the Egyptian queen. But once assured of her sincerity, Suppiluliuma sent his son Zannanza to Egypt to conclude the marriage, which would have enhanced Hittite power and prestige in the ancient Near East. However, Zannanza was murdered on the way to Egypt, dashing the possibility of an Egyptian-Hittite alliance. Despite this setback, the Hittites solidified their control over northern Syria and their client states there, in part by destroying the Hurrian kingdom of Mitanni, thereby ushering in a true Hittite Empire. This did not mean the end of dissension, however, and the Hittites were faced with regular revolts requiring a military response.

Perhaps more important, Hatti's growing political and military power brought it into direct conflict with Egypt over control of Syria. During the Amarna period under Akhenaten and his son Tutankhamun, Egypt had been focused inward, but with the rise of the Nineteenth Dynasty the Hittites came into conflict with the Egyptians. The events leading up to their clash with Ramesses II and the details of the battle itself were discussed in Chapter 2, and the result was a return to the status quo but with a peace treaty between the two kingdoms, followed by the marriage of a Hittite princess and Ramesses II.

In contrast to the now friendly relations with Egypt, Hatti experienced ongoing military problems with the Assyrians to the east and with its own subjects, resulting in a variety of rebellions. Added to this was internal political strife, including a coup and frequent rival claimants to the throne. The situation was further aggravated by persistent droughts that affected the harvests; with the land of Hatti dependent on imported grain for food, the general populace was often starving. Eventually, many peasants simply abandoned their homes, further weakening the country. As a result, Hatti's military strength began to decline, and the country was unable to withstand the assaults of the various groups known collectively as the Sea Peoples. Most likely originating in the Aegean, these people also experienced the effects of the droughts that had weakened Hatti and left their homes in a mass migration along the Mediterranean coast, fighting the local populations as they went. They reached as far as Egypt, where they were repulsed by Ramesses III. At least one group, the Peleset, then settled along the coast of Canaan, where they were known as the Philistines.

At the same time that the Sea Peoples were doing military damage during their passage through Hatti land, the Hittites' old enemies in neighboring lands took advantage of the situation and decided to attack as well. The result was that by 1180 B.C.E. the Hittite Empire was no more. In its place were smaller states, both in Anatolia and in the former Hittite territories of northern Syria, that continued Hittite traditions for a few more centuries. The most important of these Neo-Hittite kingdoms in Syria were Carchemish in the north and Hamath in the south. However, they were never united, and one by one they fell to the Assyrians during the Ninth and Eighth Centuries B.C.E.

## Hittites in the Bible

Hittites are mentioned in the First Testament in two main contexts. The first is as native inhabitants of the land of Canaan. In Genesis 23 Abraham buys the cave of Machpelah from Hittites or, more literally, "the children of Heth," who is named as a son of Canaan (Gen 10:15; 1 Chron 1:13). Similarly, Rebekah is concerned that Jacob will marry "one of these women" (literally, "a daughter of Heth"; Gen 27:46) like his brother, Esau, did (Gen 26:34; 36:2). A number of individuals are identified in Genesis as Hittites: Ephron (Gen 23:10), his father, Zohar (Gen 25:9), Beeri (Gen 26:34), and Elon (Gen 36:2). Various passages list Hittites as one of the many groups living in the land at the time of the Exodus. A good example is Deut 7:1, which mentions "the Hittites, the Girgashites, the Amorites, the Canaanites, the Perizzites, the Hivites, and the Jebusites" (see also Exod 3:8, 17; 13:5).

These references are problematic, however, because there is no evidence from either literary records or archaeological remains that the Hittites ever extended their influence that far south, to say nothing of actually living in the area. It is more likely that they have been linked to a second set of texts that refer to the Neo-Hittite states of Syria that emerged after the collapse of the Hittite Empire. Hamath in particular is frequently mentioned as marking the northern boundary of Israelite territory (e.g., Num 34:7-9; Josh 13:5; Ezek 47:16), and its king sent his son to congratulate David on his victory over the Arameans (2 Sam 8:9-10). Similarly, Josh 1:4 sets the boundaries of the land given to the Israelites: "From the wilderness and the Lebanon as far as the great river, the river Euphrates, all the land of the Hittites, to the Great Sea in the west shall be your territory." Solomon exported chariots to these "kings of the Hittites," alongside the Arameans (1 Kings 10:29; 2 Chron 1:17), and concluded diplomatic marriages with "Hittite women" (1 Kings 11:1) from those states. About a century later, the Arameans lifted a siege of Samaria after hearing the sound of many chariots and concluding that "the king of Israel has hired the kings of the Hittites and the kings of Egypt to fight against us" (2 Kings 7:6). The Greek translation of 2 Sam 24:6 refers to "Qadesh, the land of the Hittites" rather than the Hebrew reading of "the land of Tahtim Hodshi" in connection with David's census.

The chronological setting of these texts during the monarchy indicates that they refer to the Neo-Hittite states of Syria rather than the earlier Hittite Empire. The Assyrians referred to the area west of the Euphrates River as Hatti, which by the Seventh Century B.C.E. lost any ethnic meaning at all. It seems that the biblical authors identified their contemporary northern neighbors as part of the original inhabitants of Canaan. The usage may draw upon Assyrian attitudes toward those neighbors. Sargon II called the Neo-Hittite states, including Hamath, "wicked Hittites," and this negative use of *Hittite* is reflected in Ezekiel's derogatory remark that Jerusalem's mother was Hittite (Ezek 16:3, 45). The same rhetorical intent may be at play in listing the Hittites as one of the "wicked people" who had to be driven out of the land.

# Biblical Parallels

There are a number of parallels between Hittite literature, religion, and culture and the First Testament. Due to the time and distance between the Hittite Empire and the composition of the biblical texts, in most cases this is probably not the result of direct influence. Many of these parallels simply indicate similar customs and practices. For instance, like the Code of Hammurabi, the Hittite Law Code contains a series of case laws, indicating the remedy in different situations. Not only is the format of such laws comparable to many in the Bible, but in some cases there is a remarkable similarity in content. In the case of a murder in the countryside where the assailant is unknown, one is to determine the distance to the nearest town in order to assess responsibility, just as in Deut 21:1-2. Like Exod 21:18-19, Hittite law requires that someone who injures another must pay for his medical treatment and compensate him for lost income while recovering. Hittite law holds a woman who was raped in the countryside innocent, but one raped in the city was considered responsible and put to death, probably due to the assumption that she failed to cry for help; the same distinction is made in Deut 22:23-27, where the reason is stated explicitly. Another similarity is the possibility that a man would marry a relative's widow, which is comparable to the levirate marriage in Deut 25:5-6.

Some Hittite religious practices also parallel Israelite ones. The sacred areas of Hittite temples were guarded by sentries under the direction of a priest, comparable to the activity of Levites (Num 3:6-10, 32, 38; 16:9; 18:2-4, 26-28; 2 Kings 10:24). The Hebrew word for a foreign priest, *kōmer*, parallels the Hittite *kumra* for a cult official. An individual presenting a sacrifice would put his hand on the animal to indicate it was his and the sacrifice was for his benefit (Lev 1:4; 3:2, 8, 13; etc.). The Hittites also had various purification rituals that demonstrate some parallels with biblical traditions, including the use of birds to remove evil in the case of the Hittites or impurity in Lev 14:2-7, 48-53. One Hittite text describes how rams are driven into the countryside as an offering to the gods in order to eliminate a plague. This is obviously similar to the annual scapegoat ritual on the Day of Atonement described in Leviticus 16, in which the sins of the people are symbolically transferred to a goat, which is then driven into the wilderness to Azazel. Insight into Azazel's nature may be gained from other Hittite purification rituals containing the word *azuzḫi* and from a sacrificial text describing animals as *azazḫum* offerings to appease the gods. The first part of both words contains the root ʿzz, meaning "to be angry," in which case Azazel would mean "angry god." This suggests that the ritual has its origins in an attempt to appease a wilderness demon. Finally, the biblical *teraphim* may be related to the Hittite *tarpi*, referring to a spirit that could be either good or evil depending on the circumstances.

Hittite scapegoat rituals shed light on certain events in the biblical texts. For instance, a woman transfers evil onto a mouse, which she then sets free. This is reminiscent of the action of the Philistines in 1 Samuel 5–6: after they capture the ark of the Lord, a plague of tumors breaks out in their camp, so they place the ark on a cart along with golden tumors and mice and send it back to Israelite territory. The Hittite text clarifies that the mice are symbolically meant to carry away the sickness the Philistines have experienced. Similarly, in the Hittite Ritual of Samuha, curses spoken to a deity are removed by sending gold and silver images of the curses down the river to the deity in question. The casting of the metal into images of what is being removed clarifies the golden tumors made by the Philistines. Yet another means used by the Hittites to remove evils was to seal them in lead containers and send them into enemy territory. This is reflected when the prophet Zechariah sees a large container with a woman inside named "Wickedness" (Zech 5:5-11). Winged women (compare the use of birds in other Hittite rituals) appear and carry the container to Babylon, thereby eliminating Judah's sins.

Another ritual sheds light on the story of Jacob at the Jabbok River (Gen 32:22-32). While spending the night there he encounters a "man" who wrestles with him throughout the night. As daybreak approaches, the "man" asks Jacob to release him, but he refuses until the "man" blesses him. To this we can compare a Hittite festival that called for the king to hold the statue of the goddess Hebat until she blessed him. The parallels support the view that the "man" was a supernatural being, perhaps the guardian of the river.

In 1 Samuel 28 Saul consulted the dead Samuel through a woman at Endor, who communicated through a ghost (Heb. '*ôb*; cf. Isa 29:4—"your voice shall come from the ground like the voice of a ghost ['*ôb*]"). The same Hebrew word is used for a "medium" in Lev 20:27. Related to this, the Hittite cognate word *ābi* refers to a hole in the ground through which necromancers consulted underground spirits and ghosts.

The Legend of Zalpa provides better insight into the references to three of the six minor leaders in the book of Judges. In the Hittite story, the queen of Kanes bears thirty sons in one year. She sets them in baskets on the river, which takes them down to Zalpa on the seacoast. There, the gods retrieve them and raise them. Once they are grown, they return with one or more donkeys to Kanes, where their mother has given birth to thirty daughters in their absence. The gods prevent the sons and mother from recognizing each other, and the men wind up marrying their sisters. The number thirty, which is an unusual number of descendants in biblical tradition, is nonetheless repeated in connection with donkeys in the stories of Jair of Gilead, who had thirty sons who rode donkeys (Judg 10:3-4), and Abdon of Pirathon, who had forty sons and thirty grandsons, who all rode donkeys (Judg 12:13-14). Similarly, Ibzan of Bethlehem had thirty sons and thirty daughters and ensured that both groups married outside their clan (Judg 12:8-9). All three references are linked by connecting the judge to a town or region, as in the Zalpa legend, whereas two other minor judges are associated with a tribe: Tola from Issachar (Judg 10:1) and Elon from Zebulun (Judg 12:11). Moreover, by ensuring that both his thirty male and his thirty female children marry outside their clan, Ibzan goes out of his way to avoid the incestuous unions in the Zalpa legend.

A significant point of comparison between Hittite and biblical texts is the similarity of Hittite vassal treaties and the formulation of some covenant texts. Treaties between the Hittite emperors (suzerains) and their vassals use a common pattern, usually (but not always) in the same order, consisting of the following six elements:

1. *Preamble*: identifies the suzerain and gives his titles.

2. *Historical prologue*: traces the past involvement of the parties, with an emphasis on the suzerain's goodness toward the vassal and his country.

3. *Stipulations*: spell out the actual requirements of the treaty, specifying the obligations of both parties. Among other things, the suzerain promises to protect the vassal, and the vassal promises exclusive loyalty to the suzerain.

4. *Preservation of the treaty* (and regular reading): ensures that the treaty is deposited in the temple of both nations and read at regular intervals.

5. *Witnesses*: are the gods of both nations, who are listed as witnesses to the treaty and called upon to enforce the blessings and curses that follow.

6. *Curses and blessings*: state the positive consequences if the treaty is observed and the negative effects if it is broken.

A number of biblical texts dealing with the covenant relationship between Yahweh and Israel seem to be based on this pattern to varying degrees. For example, in the Ten Commandments, the phrase "I am the LORD your God" (Exod 20:2a) corresponds to the treaty preamble while "who brought you out of the land of Egypt, out of the house of slavery" (v. 2b) presents God's past dealings with the Egyptians (a historical prologue). The Ten Commandments can easily be seen as stipulations, along with the other commandments that follow in Exodus, Leviticus, and Numbers. The pattern breaks off after the Ten Commandments are listed, but some of the elements can be found elsewhere in the Pentateuch. Exodus 24:3-4, 7-8 echoes the call to preserve a treaty while Leviticus 26 contains a series of blessings (vv. 1-13) and curses (vv. 14-33). The only item missing is the witnesses, but these can be found in Deuteronomy, the core of which reflects all six elements:

1. *Preamble*: references throughout the book to "the LORD your God"

2. *Historical prologue*: chapters 1–4

3. *Stipulations*: chapters 5–26

4. *Preservation of the treaty* (and regular reading): Deut 10:1-5; 27:2-3; 31:9-13, 24-26

5. *Witnesses*: Deut 4:26; 31:19-22, 26-28; 32:39-43 (note that "gods" are not witnesses)

6. *Curses and blessings*: chapters 27–28

While Exodus through Numbers, as well as Deuteronomy, can be understood much like an actual treaty, the treaty elements can also be adapted into a narrative context, as with the description of the covenant ceremony in Joshua 24. Verse 2a ("Thus says Yahweh, the God of Israel") presents the Lord's name and title. Verses 2b-13 trace the past involvements (= the historical prologue) of the two parties, reviewing the history of the patriarchs, the exodus, the wilderness period, and the conquest, and the people echo this in verses 17-18. The stipulation in verse 14 that they give exclusive fidelity to Yahweh is repeated as a command in verse 23 after the people assert their desire to serve Yahweh. This single element was undoubtedly developed by the "statutes and ordinances" mentioned in verse 25. The covenant is written down in verses 25-26a; the text does not say it is deposited in the sanctuary (there is no indication that the stone in v. 26b contained the words of the covenant), although that is a likely assumption, especially if "the book of the law of God" refers to the "book of the law" that Moses deposited in the "ark of the covenant of Yahweh" (Deut 31:24-26). There is no provision for regular reading in Joshua 24, but the command in Josh 1:8 ("This book of the law shall not depart out of your mouth; you shall meditate on it day and night") would have that effect (see also Deut 31:10-13). The people themselves (Josh 24:22) and the stone erected in the sanctuary (vv. 26b-27) are named as witnesses to the covenant. Once again, there are no divine witnesses, since this would violate the spirit of the proposed covenant, with its call that they worship only Yahweh. Yahweh's punishment if they break the covenant (vv. 19-20) parallels a treaty's curses in which the gods inflict harm. There are no explicit blessings, although the historical prologue gave evidence of Yahweh's past blessing, which could be expected to continue if they are faithful. It is impossible to prove that this chapter is based on a suzerainty treaty (i.e., that one was actually used during composition of this passage), but the points of contact are too numerous and significant to be the result of chance. Thus the ancient treaty form is a useful model for interpreting the chapter.

It was once thought that the points of contact with Hittite vassal treaties meant that the concept of a covenant, and perhaps even the texts themselves, must date to the time of the Hittite treaties. However, this idea fails to allow for the possibility that an awareness of the treaty format continued after the last such treaty. Moreover, first-millennium Assyrian vassal treaties were subsequently discovered that show an even closer connection with the biblical texts in two important ways. First, whereas the curse section in Hittite treaties is brief, the Assyrian treaties develop the curses at much greater length; Esarhaddon's vassal treaties contain 250 lines of curses. As such, the latter are much closer to what we find in Lev 26:14-33 and Deuteronomy 27–28. Second, while the content of some biblical curses, such as drought, illness, destruction of a city, and cannibalism (Deut 28:23-24, 27, 52-53), can be found in both Hittite and Assyrian treaties, others like blindness, slavery, and locusts (Deut 28:28, 32, 38) are found only in Assyrian treaties.

Nonetheless, there are also features of the Hittite treaties that are not found in the Assyrian ones but are reflected in the biblical covenantal texts. Perhaps the most significant is the historical prologue, which details the suzerain's past benevolence. In addition, only the Hittite treaties include blessings. Moreover, whatever the historical reality might have been, the Hittite treaties give the vassals a choice whether to accept the treaty, just as Yahweh does with the Israelites. Finally, the Hittite treaties define state boundaries, giving land to those who obey and removing it from those who do not, yet another concept found in the biblical covenant. In light of this, the most likely explanation is that the biblical texts are most directly influenced by the Assyrian treaties, which date from a time much closer to the composition of the former, while at the same time preserving an echo of the Hittite treaties, perhaps mediated through their Neo-Hittite neighbors to the north.

A final Hittite text to note is a myth discovered at Bogazköy that clearly reflects a West Semitic context. It deals with the god Elkunirša and his wife, Ashertu, plus the storm god and his sister. *Elkunirša* means "El, creator of the earth," a formula found in Canaanite inscriptions as well as Gen 14:19, while Ashertu corresponds to Athirat, El's wife at Ugarit, as well as the biblical Asherah. In that context, the storm god is obviously Ba'al, and his sister is Anat. The text describes how Ashertu propositions Baʿal, but when he rejects her, she denounces him to her husband. El and Ashertu then conspire against Baʿal, but Anat learns of their plans and warns him. After a lengthy gap, the text resumes with a description of an injured Baʿal being treated. To date, no parallels to this myth have been found in West Semitic texts, but the characters are major players in the Ugaritian literature and, with the possible exception of Anat, are also found in the biblical literature. Nonetheless, the basic plot is reflected in the Egyptian "Tale of Two Brothers" as well as the story of Joseph and Potiphar's wife (see Chapter 2).

# CHAPTER 4

# Persia

## The Seventh–Sixth Centuries

The core territory of ancient Persia is known today as Iran. The region was first united by the Median king Cyaxares (625–585 B.C.E.), who combined his own lands in the northern area with those of his Persian vassals to the south. Cyaxares defeated the Assyrians at Ashshur in 614 B.C.E., then allied himself with the Babylonians to conquer Nineveh in 612 B.C.E., thus effectively ending the Assyrian Empire. With their spoils from the Assyrian Empire, the Medians added the mountains of Anatolia and parts of northern Syria to their territory of western Iran and as far east as modern Tehran. Cyaxares was succeeded by his son Astyages (585–550 B.C.E.), who sought to solidify his relationship with the Persians by marrying his daughter Mandane to Cambyses I (who ruled Persia proper, ca. 600–559 B.C.E.). Their union produced a son, Cyrus II, who would eventually be known as Cyrus the Great. Six years after assuming the Persian throne upon his father's death, Cyrus rebelled against his grandfather Astyages. After three years of fighting, Astyages was abandoned by his own forces, and Cyrus took over the Median Empire in 550 B.C.E., but allowed Astyages to live. This move was in keeping with his general benevolence to defeated enemies and his desire to use local personages to administer his empire. Although Astyages was kept at Cyrus's court, many other Medes were given positions in the Persian bureaucracy.

When Croesus, the king of Lydia and Astyages' brother-in-law, attacked in 547 B.C.E., Cyrus easily defeated him and added Asia Minor to his realm. After solidifying his hold on that region and expanding his empire eastward as far as northwestern India, Cyrus focused on the Babylonians on the other side of the Tigris River. The Persian forces invaded in 539 B.C.E., and after routing the Babylonian army at Opis, north of Babylon, the Persians took the capital city without a battle. Some sources indicate that the citizens welcomed Cyrus as a liberator who restored the worship of Marduk that the Babylonian emperor Nabonidus had demoted. Through his capture of the Babylonian capital and its ruler, Cyrus now inherited the entire Neo-Babylonian Empire, including the lands of Israel and Judah, although the extent of his direct control may have been limited at this point.

Shortly after taking possession of the city of Babylon, Cyrus issued a decree calling for the return of cult items that had been taken from various Mesopotamian sanctuaries by the Babylonians. This edict is preserved in the Cyrus Cylinder that was discovered in the ruins of Babylon in 1879; the relevant portion reads as follows:

> From [Babylon] to Ashshur and (from) Susa, Agade, Eshnunna, Zamban, Me-Turnu, Der, as far as the region of Gutium, the sacred centers on the other side of the Tigris, whose sanctuaries had been abandoned for a long time, I returned the images of the gods, who had resided there, to their places and I let them dwell in eternal abodes. I gathered all their inhabitants and returned to them their dwellings. In addition, at the command of Marduk, the great lord, I settled in their habitations, in pleasing abodes, the gods of Sumer and Akkad, whom Nabonidus, to the anger of the lord of the gods, had brought into Babylon.

Scholars often compare this passage to Ezra 6:3-5, part of a larger section of the book preserved in Aramaic, which claims to preserve a decree from Cyrus that explicitly provides for the reconstruction of the Jerusalem temple to be paid by the royal treasury and for the sacred vessels taken during Nebuchadnezzar's destruction of Jerusalem to be returned. Although the wording differs from Cyrus's cylinder, the general content of Ezra 6:3-5 is usually considered to be historically accurate, in part because it deals only with the rebuilding of the Temple and the restoration of related sacred items, with no reference to a wholesale return of the deportees.

In contrast, Ezra 1:2-4 (cf. 2 Chron 36:23) has Cyrus attribute his decision to Yahweh's direct inspiration and includes permission for all those deported fifty years earlier to return to Jerusalem; the following verses even include a statement that Cyrus himself gave them the temple vessels (Ezra 1:7). This presentation of Cyrus as acting under Yahweh's direction is paralleled by Isa 45:1, which proclaims Cyrus to be Yahweh's "anointed" (i.e., his Messiah). Ezra 1–2 provides a census of those who returned under the leadership of Sheshbazzar, "the prince of Judah" (Ezra 1:8), totaling some 42,360 individuals (Ezra 2:64), with the detailed enumeration by households being repeated in Neh 7:6-73. However, a blanket amnesty is not actually announced in the Cyrus Cylinder, since the statement quoted above that "I gathered all their inhabitants and returned to them their dwellings" refers only to peoples within Mesopotamia and does not envision a wide-scale relocation of previous displaced populations. Nevertheless, some people would be needed to transport the temple vessels back to Jerusalem and, by implication, to oversee the Temple's reconstruction. The best explanation, therefore, is that the list in Ezra 2 // Nehemiah 7 is an attempt to link the subsequent population of Judah with the return while also suggesting multiple migrations over time.

Many deportees would have chosen to stay in Mesopotamia. Most, if not all, of them would have been born there after the deportation and therefore had never seen Judah or Jerusalem. Babylon was their home, and the majority would not be eager to leave a settled, relatively comfortable, and secure lifestyle for a country and a city they had never seen, especially one that had been devastated by war. That does not mean that they would not support those who chose to make the long, difficult journey: Ezra 1:5-6 notes how they gave money, jewels, and gold to those "whose spirit God had stirred" to return, but they were not willing to join them. As a result, many stayed behind and continued to develop the roots they had established in exile. One consequence is that business documents from Nippur a century later reveal that a major banking family there had Jewish names, as did many of their clients.

Cyrus's decree once again reflects his typical attitude toward conquered territories, including their religious systems, while the biblical assertions that the initial returnees were led by a member of the royal family, namely, Sheshbazzar, is consistent with the Persian policy of appointing local persons with some established stature as regional representatives of Persian authority. Restoring the Temple would have solicited the support of the inhabitants of Judah, now called Yehud, for Persian authority in the area. Local goodwill was important in the absence of any military presence for at least a decade, until Cyrus's son Cambyses II captured Egypt in 525 B.C.E. In the interim, governors appointed from among the local leaders represented Persian rule in the region. Thus, the first such leader was Sheshbazzar, sent from Babylon as the leader of a first small group of returnees; but apart from laying the foundations for the Temple (Ezra 5:14-16), we have no record of his activities.

Cyrus died in battle in the East in 530 B.C.E. and was followed by his son Cambyses II, who continued to expand the empire, subduing Egypt in 525 B.C.E. He died, perhaps killing himself, in Syria in 522 B.C.E. on his way back to Persia to deal with his brother Bardiya's usurpation of the throne. The latter was quickly killed by Darius I, one of Cambyses' generals. Darius then faced a series of revolts throughout the empire, resulting in nineteen battles during his first year of rule. His succession struggles are commemorated in the Behistun inscription, carved one hundred meters up a cliff face and measuring fifteen meters high by twenty-five meters wide. It consists of parallel columns in Elamite, Old Persian, and Babylonian and played a major role in deciphering the latter language and all the Mesopotamian texts that used it, and from there the Assyrian and Sumerian cuneiform texts. After suppressing the initial revolts, Darius continued to expand the Persian Empire through invasions of Scythia, north of the Black Sea, and Greece. However, his forces were defeated at Marathon in 490 B.C.E., and he died four years later before he was able to mount another attempt to subdue Greece.

In the meantime, Sheshbazzar was followed by Zerubbabel, another member of the royal family, accompanied by Joshua as

high priest. We do not know exactly when he arrived from
Babylon, but references to him in the books of Haggai and
Zechariah indicate that he was present in Jerusalem in 520 B.C.E.
(see especially the dates in Hag 1:1; 2:1, 20) and resumed construction of the Temple (e.g., Zech 4:8). Unfortunately, we have no
other information about him, especially how long he served as
governor or when and why his term ended. There are indications
in the books of Haggai and Zechariah that those prophets may
have seen him as a potential Davidic king who would replace
rather than just administer Persian control of the land. For the
most part, Zechariah expresses such hopes in a subdued way,
using the code term *branch* or *shoot* in 3:8 and 6:12, a term with
kingly associations probably well-known among the returnees
(see Isa 4:2; 11:1; Jer 23:5) but less likely so by the Persian over-
lords. However, the explicit references to Zerubbabel in 4:6-10
indicate the contemporary understanding of the nature and role of
Zerubbabel in the divine plan. The prophet Haggai was bolder
than his contemporary, stating in Hag 2:21-23:

> Speak to Zerubbabel, governor of Judah, saying, I am about to
> shake the heavens and the earth, and to overthrow the throne of
> kingdoms; I am about to destroy the strength of the kingdoms of
> the nations, and overthrow the chariots and their riders; and the
> horses and their riders shall fall, every one by the sword of a com-
> rade. On that day, says the LORD of hosts, I will take you, O
> Zerubbabel my servant, son of Shealtiel, says the LORD, and make
> you like a signet ring; for I have chosen you, says the LORD of hosts.

Such a pronouncement made as part of a prophecy of political
upheaval may have been the catalyst for the Persians to remove
Zerubbabel as governor, or he may simply have faded into political and historical obscurity.

# The Fifth Century

The biblical material says nothing about the period after
Zerubbabel until the arrival of Nehemiah in 445 B.C.E., corresponding with the twentieth year of Artaxerxes I (Neh 2:1). However,
we know that Darius had built upon the work of his predecessors

to reorganize the Persian Empire into twenty regions, called satrapies, each with an administrator called a satrap, and had a system of roads constructed to facilitate ease of movement throughout the empire. Judah was part of the fifth satrapy, called "Across the River," which encompassed Phoenicia, Cyprus, and Syria and included a number of smaller provinces whose governors reported to the satrap. Archaeological finds such as seals, bullae, and jar handles refer to a number of governors in the area during the Persian period, and at least three of them—Elnathan, Yehoezer, and Ahzai—have recognizably Jewish names, indicating that Persia continued to appoint local individuals as governors, although there is insufficient information to assess their status within the Yehud community prior to their appointment.

There are some hints that Nehemiah was also a member of the royal family. Although it is impossible to be certain as to his ancestry, his reference to Jerusalem as "the city, the place of my ancestors' graves" (Neh 2:3, 5) strongly suggests a royal lineage, since only the kings were buried within the city itself. Such a family background is consistent with the Persian practice of using native royalty as administrators so as to legitimate their own rule, and it gives a measure of credence to the accusation of kingly pretensions in Neh 6:6-7. Certainly, his actions in rebuilding the city and the Temple and enacting social justice (Nehemiah 5) are consonant with the royal role envisioned by prophets such as Ezekiel and Haggai. Moreover, his arrival in Yehud coincided with significant political developments in the area. Xerxes I (486–465 B.C.E.), son of Darius, was unsuccessful in the effort to pacify Greece, and the Persians ultimately withdrew from Europe. Under his successor, Artaxerxes I (464–424 B.C.E.), Egypt revolted in 460 B.C.E. with help from the Athenians, and it took the Persians six years to suppress that uprising. In 449 B.C.E., the satrap of "Across the River" himself rebelled, although he was reconciled with the emperor within a year. Thus, Nehemiah's arrival in Judah came just after a lengthy period of unrest, first in Egypt and then in the much larger region. By appointing a member of the royal line as governor of Judah, Artaxerxes was probably trying to solicit goodwill in what at that point was a strategic border area.

Despite the threat of armed attack, Nehemiah rebuilt the city walls (Neh 4:13-23), which enhanced administration and trade. He sought to regularize local religious practices in keeping with Jewish practices in Babylon, including restoring the sanctity of the Sabbath by forcibly preventing commerce on that day (Neh 13:15-21). Nehemiah worked for unity among Jews from different economic levels by canceling all debts, although he did not redistribute the land, and presented himself as a model by not claiming his own living allowance. He also opposed mixed marriages as a threat to religious purity (Neh 13:23-29), although there was also a political factor in that he was opposed by enemies from nearby countries, such as Sanballat, the governor of Samaria (Neh 3:33-42 [Eng 4:1-9]).

# The Fourth Century

The next major development in Judah was the arrival of Ezra "the scribe" from Mesopotamia. According to Ezra 7, he was commissioned by Artaxerxes to establish "the law" of God as the legal rule for Palestine (vv. 12-26). The text does not specify which of the three Artaxerxes this was, but the likely candidate is Artaxerxes II (404–358 B.C.E.); Ezra's arrival in Jerusalem during the seventh year of his reign (Ezra 7:7) would correspond to 398/397 B.C.E. As with Nehemiah, this date is significant in light of regional developments. In 404 B.C.E. Egypt succeeded in throwing off Persian control and retained its independence for the next sixty years. The Egyptians also sent military incursions along the Mediterranean coast, as far north as Phoenicia. Against this backdrop, establishing Jewish law for the land of Judah parallels the codification of Egyptian law sponsored by Darius I a century earlier. Just as that earlier effort was done to win the favor and support of the local populace, so too Ezra's promulgation of the law of God under Persian sponsorship would have the same end, namely, to win support from the inhabitants of an area of the empire that was being threatened. The exact nature of this law, which he read in a public ceremony (Neh 8:1-3), is disputed, but the scholarly consensus is that it comprised a form of the Pentateuch close to—if not identical with—what we have today. This had the effect of reorganizing the community along religious lines and laid the foundations for Judaism as "a religion of the book."

But religious uniformity was not shared by all Jews, especially those living outside Judah. This is demonstrated from Aramaic documents found at Elephantine, an island in the upper Nile at Aswan, just below the first cataract, marking Egypt's southern boundary. The island contained a colony of Jewish soldiers in the service of the pharaoh, along with their families, whose date of arrival there is uncertain. In any case, the documents found there indicate that they were well established, with a functioning temple to Yahweh, whom they called Yahu, when Cambyses II conquered Egypt in 525 B.C.E. In 410 B.C.E. that temple was destroyed by Egyptian priests of Khnum. Consequently, the Jewish residents of Elephantine wrote letters to various individuals in Syro-Palestine, including Bagoas, the governor of Judah; Deliah and Shelemiah, sons of Sanballat of Samaria (cf. Neh 2:19); Johanan, the high priest of Jerusalem (Neh 12:23); and other Judean priests and nobles. Both Bagoas and Deliah responded positively. This indicates that the centralization of worship at the Jerusalem Temple was not universally accepted outside Judah or even by all within the land, but the agreement by those in Elephantine to present only grain offerings and not animal sacrifice may be an attempt to render it more palatable. The inhabitants of Elephantine certainly considered themselves observant Jews, since a papyrus from them provides details for calculating the date of Passover as well as the purity rituals to follow in celebrating it. Nonetheless, they were also polytheistic, listing among their gods Anat, Bethel, and even the combined deities Anat-Yahu and Anat-Bethel. In other words, in addition to the issue of a temple outside Jerusalem, they did not share the monotheistic views that had taken root in Jerusalem.

An Aramaic version of the Behistun inscription was also found at Elephantine, as well as the earliest known copy of the teachings of Ahiqar. Ahiqar was an Assyrian official serving Sennacherib and Esarhaddon (and Tobit's nephew, according to Tob 1:22), who adopted his nephew Nadin and trained him as his own replacement. Nadin denounced Ahiqar as a traitor and convinced the king to kill him, but the executioner spared his life because Ahiqar had done the same for him some years earlier, substituting the body of another prisoner. The Elephantine papyrus contains a number of wisdom sayings as Ahiqar's actual instructions to his nephew. As is often the case with wisdom texts, the general concern for using proper speech, acting appropriately at the royal court, showing respect for parents, and so on, parallels many examples of Wisdom literature from the ancient Near East, including biblical ones. More specifically, although the precise descriptions are different, personified Wisdom in Ahiqar is paralleled by Lady Wisdom in Prov 8:22-31. At times, the wording of individual sayings comes close to matching. The best example is saying 3 in Ahiqar (vi:81): "Spare the rod / Spoil the child," which can be compared with Prov 13:24: "Those who spare the rod hate their children, / but those who love them are diligent to discipline them" (cf. 19:18; 23:13-14). Taken all together, the affinities between the teachings of Ahiqar and biblical wisdom texts show once again that the biblical writers were sharing in a much wider tradition than that of ancient Israel alone.

After the time of Ezra, there is no reference in any biblical texts to the Persian Empire and its impact on Judah, nor do Persian documents pay any special attention to the region. The Persian Empire experienced a large number of internal revolts during the Fourth Century B.C.E., and Egypt enjoyed a lengthy period of independence during the same period. Then, just as Darius III (reigned 336–330 B.C.E.) managed to subdue Egypt yet again, Alexander the Great of Macedonia entered Asia Minor at the head of a Greek army. After the armies of the local satrapies failed to repel the invaders, Darius assembled the imperial army, but he was defeated at Issus in 333 B.C.E. and forced to abandon much of his family as he retreated. Alexander then moved south through Syria, and apart from resistance by Tyre and Gaza, he passed through the region unopposed; Jerusalem greeted him with open gates, and Egypt welcomed him as a liberator. Although it would be another three years before Alexander took control of the Persian homeland, and three more before he eliminated all resistance and continued his march to the banks of the Indus River, from 332 B.C.E. onward Judah was under the control of the Greeks.

# Influence on the Bible?

There is no evidence of any significant Persian influence on the content of the books of the First Testament. While Ezra and Nehemiah report historical matters involving the Persians, the literary style is consistent with other biblical historical books in general and the book of Chronicles in particular, and similar historical notations in Haggai and Zechariah also reflect Israelite contexts. The book of Esther is set during the reign of Xerxes I (called Ahasuerus in the book), that is, the mid-Fifth Century B.C.E., but the work is actually a fictional account of the origins of the Jewish festival of Purim and dates from the middle of the Second Century B.C.E. There are a few hints of Persian impact on the book of Qoheleth. First of all, there are two Persian loan words in the book: *pardēs* (park) in 2:5 and *pitgām* (decree) in 8:11, indicating some minor linguistic influence. In addition, Qoh 5:8 states, "If you see in a province the oppression of the poor and the violation of justice and right, do not be amazed at the matter; for the high official is watched by a higher, and there are yet higher ones over them," which sounds like a description of the Persian bureaucratic system rising from provinces through the satrapies to the emperor himself and may also hint at the Persian officials who reported directly to the king on the activities of the satraps and regional governors. The latter individuals may also be reflected in the satan's statements that he has come "from going to and fro on the earth, and from walking up and down on it" (Job 1:7; 2:1) as well as his actual role of raising accusations against Job and against Joshua (Zechariah 3).

This leads to another possible point of influence not so much on the First Testament but on the later development of the concept of the devil in late Second Temple Judaism and on into Christianity. In both Job and Zechariah the Hebrew word *śāṭān* is always accompanied by the definite article, indicating that it is a common noun rather than a name, since one does not link *the* with a name. The noun *śāṭān* derives from the Hebrew verb meaning to "oppose" or "accuse," so *the śāṭān* is a title indicating what the individual does, not a name. Nor is there anything inherently evil about "the satan" in Job and Zechariah. He is merely doing his job, which is to raise accusations, much as a prosecuting attorney in a modern-day court of law. However, with the increasing emphasis on monotheism in the postexilic period, believers could no longer blame evil on other gods, and some even attributed this characteristic to Yahweh, as in Isa 45:7: "I form light and create darkness, / I make weal and create woe; / I Yahweh do all these things." Before long, however, believers developed the concept of a devil, who came to be known as Satan, to explain the negative aspects of their lives, especially the presence of evil in the world. This development was probably influenced by the dualistic nature of Zoroastrianism, the Persian religion. Central to Zoroastrianism is the belief in two deities, Ahura Mazda, the benevolent Lord of Wisdom, and the thoroughly evil Angra Mainyu, also known as Ahriman. Human existence reflects the cosmic struggle between those two opposing divine forces, although Angra Mainyu was ultimately destined to be overcome by Ahura Mazda. In the same way, Second Temple Judaism and subsequently Christianity developed the concept of Satan, the devil, as a malevolent being opposing God's goodness, but whose power is ultimately less than that of the deity and so he will eventually be defeated. As we will see in the next chapter, such a dualistic perspective is also reflected in apocalyptic literature such as Daniel 7–12, even though it was composed during the later Hellenistic period.

# CHAPTER 5

# Greece

After taking possession of Syro-Palestine and Egypt in 332 B.C.E. (see Chapter 4), Alexander the Great continued his eastward march, defeating Darius III again in Assyria in 331 B.C.E., then moving southwest to capture Babylon, Susa, and Persepolis, whereupon Darius was killed by his own satraps. Alexander continued to conquer lands farther east, but after his troops stopped at the banks of the Indus River in 326 B.C.E. and refused to go any farther, he retired to Babylon, where he died in 323 B.C.E. at the age of thirty-three. In the absence of an obvious successor, a struggle followed among Alexander's generals for control of various parts of the empire. Of these, only two are of concern for the history of Israel and Judah: Seleucus, who took control of Babylon by 312 B.C.E., and Ptolemy, who established himself in Egypt in the same year. Initially Seleucus controlled Palestine, but Ptolemy seized control of it in 301 B.C.E., with Seleucus still dominating Syria. The next century saw five wars between the Seleucids and the Ptolemies for control of Palestine. The last of these occurred in 202–195 B.C.E. when the Seleucids, taking advantage of the fact that the new Egyptian ruler Ptolemy V was just a child, finally won control of the region in 198 B.C.E.

# The Ptolemaic Period

The extant records provide no explicit testimony as to the nature of the Ptolemies' rule in Palestine, but judging from the lack of any opposition in Jewish literature, including the First Testament, it was probably relatively benign. If they organized the territory in the same way they did their other possessions, there would have been a governor with both civil and military powers. Small military garrisons were stationed in major cities during times of peace, but their numbers increased greatly during wartime. Provinces were subdivided into *hyparchies*, in which the collection of taxes, exportation of food to Egypt, and other financial affairs were overseen by the *hyparchos* and the *oikonomos*. Towns were led by a *komarch*, who worked with royal judges, called *dikastai*. Within this administrative framework, the Ptolemies usually employed local functionaries. Assuming that the administrative decree from Antiochus III in 197 B.C.E. (see further below) continued Ptolemaic practice, Jewish territory would have been a theocracy controlled by the high priest in Jerusalem.

Although the full details of all five Syrian wars between the Ptolemies and the Seleucids for control of Palestine need not concern us, since none of the battles were fought in the Jewish territory, a few events should be noted here as background for the discussion of the book of Daniel later in this chapter. The Second Syrian War (260–253 B.C.E.) was concluded with the marriage of Berenice, sister of Ptolemy III, to Antiochus II, while her murder set off the Third Syrian War (246–241 B.C.E.) in which Ptolemy advanced as far as Babylon before withdrawing. The Fourth Syrian War (219–217 B.C.E.) ended when the advancing forces of Antiochus III were stopped by Ptolemy IV at Raphia in Gaza on June 22, 217 B.C.E. The Fifth Syrian War (202–195 B.C.E.) ended with Ptolemy V marrying Antiochus III's daughter, Cleopatra I.

Despite the lack of information, we can assume that Judea experienced some degree of hellenization, that is, the influence of Greek culture and ideas during the Ptolemaic period. The Letter of Aristeas dates the Greek translation of the First Testament to the reign of Ptolemy II (283–246 B.C.E.). The translation is called the Septuagint (from the Latin *septuaginta*, "seventy") because of the legendary account that Ptolemy brought seventy scholars from

Jerusalem to Alexandria in order to prepare the work for inclusion in his library. While clearly fictional, the story indicates the predominance of the Greek language among Jews outside Palestine.

The only indication of possible hellenization in the composition of a First Testament work occurs in the book of Qoheleth. Since there is no indication of the upheaval associated with the Seleucid period in Palestine, and the sense of political stability points to the Ptolemaic period, the book probably dates from the middle of the Third Century B.C.E. In terms of Hellenistic influences, Qoh 1:4-7 has been linked to a number of schools of Greek philosophy, although not without differing from some of them as well. Because of this, it is worth quoting the passage in full for easy comparison:

> A generation goes, and a generation comes,
> but the earth remains forever.
> The sun rises and the sun goes down,
> and hurries to the place that it rises.
> The wind blows to the south,
> and goes around to the north;
> round and round goes the wind,
> and on its circuits the wind returns.
> All streams run to the sea,
> but the sea is not full;
> to the place where the streams flow,
> there they continue to flow.

The description of constant movement and change within nature in Qoh 1:4-7 is reminiscent of Heraclitus's claim that everything is in flux, especially his famous statement, "No one ever steps in the same river twice." A similar perspective, as well as Heraclitus's belief that all things can be categorized in terms of opposites, may also have influenced the pairs of opposite actions in Qoh 3:1-9 illustrating that there is "a time for every matter under heaven" (v. 1). Qoheleth 1:4-7 also reflects the cyclical understanding of life found among the Stoics, although without their deterministic understanding of the course of events. The passage also mentions three of the four elements prevalent in pre-Socratic Greek philosophy, namely, earth (v. 4), air (wind; v. 6), and water (v. 7); if one equates the sun in verse 5 with fire, then all four are listed.

There are other echoes of Greek thought elsewhere in the book. For instance, Parmenides' assertion that there is no change is echoed in Qoh 1:9:

> What has been is what will be,
> and what has been done is what will be done;
> there is nothing new under the sun.

The Epicurean insistence on pleasure is paralleled by Qoheleth's repeated call to enjoy whatever good things come in life (2:24; 3:12-13, 22; 5:17-18; 8:15; cf. 11:9), but contrary to the hedonism of Epicureanism, with one exception (3:22), Qoheleth always reminds us that any such opportunity comes from God, who will hold us responsible for how we have used that gift. Qoheleth 3:21 asks whether the human spirit goes up and that of animals goes down, suggesting an awareness of Plato's doctrine of the immortality of the soul but a reluctance to accept it. Qoheleth 7:16-18 argues against excessive righteousness, wisdom, wickedness, or folly, concluding, "It is good that you should take hold of the one, without letting go of the other," much like the golden mean of Pythagoras, Socrates, Plato, and Aristotle. Qoheleth's description of his approach to understanding as "adding one thing to another to find the sum" (7:27) reflects the inductive method used by many philosophers.

# The Seleucid Period

As noted above, Antiochus III (the Great) took control of Palestine from the Ptolemies in 198 B.C.E., after which he issued a decree confirming the administration of the territory. The land was organized into four provinces, each with a governor and troops. Judea was a subdivision of the province of Samaria that was administered by the high priest in Jerusalem, aided by a council of elders and the priests, thus constituting a limited theocracy. There is no indication that this was an innovation and probably continued the practice followed under the Ptolemies, who like the Seleucids were Greeks. Antiochus invaded Greece itself in 192 B.C.E. but was forced back to Anatolia by the Romans the following year and beaten by them again at Magnesia in 190 B.C.E. The peace treaty restricted him to the territory east of Tarsus and imposed war reparations of three thousand talents, plus an additional one thousand talents a year for twelve years. According to 2 Maccabees 3, in order to make those payments, his son and successor, Seleucus IV (187–175 B.C.E.), sent his court official Heliodorus to seize the temple treasury in Jerusalem, but he failed after being opposed by a gold-clad rider on a horse. Despite the fanciful elements of this account, its historical basis is demonstrated by correspondence with Heliodorus that outlines the contemporary Seleucid policy of taking over sanctuaries in order to gain access to their money supply. Heliodorus eventually assassinated Seleucus, who was replaced by the latter's brother, Antiochus IV (175–164 B.C.E.). He had pretensions of divinity and took the title Epiphanes, meaning "(god) manifest," although some called him Epimanes (the mad one).

The relationship between the Judeans and their Seleucid rulers changed drastically during the reign of Antiochus. Seeing Hellenism as a way to unify his entire kingdom, he began to promote it aggressively and even imposed it in places where it had not taken hold, such as Judea in general and Jerusalem in particular. Some Jerusalemites supported this, and Joshua, going by the name Jason, bribed Antiochus to replace his brother Onias III as high priest, a position that was supposed to be hereditary and passed on only when a current officeholder died. Jason built a gymnasium and organized advanced physical training for Jewish males. Since Greek athletics were traditionally conducted nude, some Jews went to great lengths to hide their circumcision, which Greeks considered barbaric self-mutilation, with some going so far as to sew on fresh skin. Jason held the high priesthood from 174 to 171 B.C.E., when Menelaus offered Antiochus an even bigger bribe for the position. This was even more offensive to traditionalist Jews since Menelaus was not of the proper priestly lineage of Zadok, and the situation was further aggravated when he began to use the temple treasury for his own purposes.

In 170 B.C.E. the regents of the sixteen-year-old Ptolemy VI declared war on Antiochus, who invaded Egypt a year later and quickly defeated the opposing forces. Erroneously believing that Antiochus was dead, Jason attacked Jerusalem and besieged Menelaus in the city citadel, whereupon Antiochus withdrew from Egypt to deal with this rebellion, slaughtering much of the city's population, looting the temple, and restoring Menelaus as high priest. Antiochus returned to Egypt in 168 B.C.E. and marched on Alexandria. Along the way he met a single elderly Roman ambassador named Gaius Popillius Laenas, who informed him that if he did not withdraw, Rome would consider itself at war with him. When Antiochus asked for time to consult his advisors, Gaius drew a circle in the sand around the invader and announced that he had to answer before he stepped outside it. Antiochus had no choice but to leave Egypt, and Gaius left us with the idiom "draw a line in the sand" to indicate an ultimatum.

On his return through Judea in 167 B.C.E., Antiochus encountered hostility as a result of his earlier sack of Jerusalem and defilement of the temple, and he decided to end the problem once and for all by outlawing Judaism. His chief tax collector led an attack against Jerusalem on a Sabbath, butchering the males, taking the women and children as slaves, and installing a garrison in the fortress Akra next to the temple. Jewish practices were forbidden: the regular sacrifices and feasts were stopped, Sabbath observance was prevented, and practicing circumcision or possessing the Pentateuch were punished by death. Pagan altars were erected throughout the land, unclean animals were sacrificed on them, and Jews were forced to eat swine. In December 167 B.C.E. sacrifices began to be offered to Zeus on a new altar in the temple. Some traditions indicate that the animal was a pig and that a statue of Zeus with Antiochus's face was also erected in the sanctuary.

Armed Jewish resistance to Antiochus's new policies began in the village of Modein, about thirty-two kilometers northwest of Jerusalem, when the priest Mattathias killed a Syrian official who was trying to make the inhabitants offer pagan sacrifices. He then overturned the altar and fled with his five sons into the hills, from where they began a campaign of guerrilla warfare. When Mattathias died a year or so later, his son Judas took over the leadership of the role. Judas was given the nickname Maccabeus (the hammer), and the revolt became known as the Maccabean revolt.

As Judas gained more support, he was able to defeat two different armies sent to capture him. Then in 164 B.C.E. the Maccabees defeated a third army and entered Jerusalem in triumph. They installed observant priests in the temple, who conducted the required purification rituals over the course of eight days. On December 15, 164 B.C.E., the temple was rededicated, an event commemorated in the Jewish feast of Hanukkah (Dedication), and the proper sacrifices resumed.

After this, the persecution ended, although the struggle for control of Judea continued for about a decade. Judas was killed in battle in 160 B.C.E. and was replaced by his brother Jonathan. Around 155 B.C.E. the Seleucids recognized Jonathan as the governor of Judea, and in 142 B.C.E. his brother Simon took advantage of conflict among the Seleucids to establish an independent Jewish kingdom that lasted until 63 B.C.E. In that year there was a brief civil war between the brothers Hyrcanus II and Aristobulus II, each of whom claimed both the kingship and the high priesthood. Both appealed to their Roman allies in the person of General Pompey, who sided with Hyrcanus and, after a three-month siege, marched into the defeated Jerusalem. Pompey affirmed Hyrcanus as high priest but not as king, instead installing Antipater of Idumea, the father of Herod the Great, to oversee Rome's political control of Judea. Since the intervening history of the Maccabean kings is not reflected in the common canon of the First Testament (the Maccabean revolt only is detailed in the deuterocanonical/ apocryphal Second Maccabees, while First Maccabees continues the story to the end of King John Hyrcanus's reign), I will not pursue it further.

On the other hand, the events leading up to the Maccabean revolt constitute the essential background for understanding the second half of the book of Daniel, which was written in the early stages of Antiochus's persecution, before the revolt started. Daniel 7–12 constitutes an *apocalypse*, a literary genre that was extremely popular from about 200 B.C.E to 200 C.E. There are dozens of examples of both Jewish and Christian apocalypses, in addition to the only two biblical examples, Daniel 7–12 and the book of Revelation in the Second Testament. It was especially popular in crisis situations, since it asserted that God would ultimately defeat the audience's oppressors. A defining characteristic of this genre was a review of historical events as if they had not yet happened, thus giving the appearance that they were predicted at some point in the past. The purpose was to gain acceptance of the apocalypse's message: if the author had been correct about what had already happened, the same must be true of the future deliverance. Yet apocalypses regularly presented their historical reviews through bizarre imagery and/or very general, allusive references to events, so that only those who knew the "code" could decipher the book. Daniel 7–12 takes this approach to the Hellenistic period in Judea. To someone without any knowledge of the history of Ptolemaic and Seleucid rule in Palestine, that section of the book is at times strange and indecipherable and at other times vague and general. But armed with an awareness of the historical background, a reader can crack the code and see that the author is using the apocalypse genre to demonstrate that the events were foreseen by God, and therefore God is in control of the situation.

This can be illustrated through an examination of the strange symbolic imagery as well as the general but allusive narration in Daniel 7–12 in light of the history outlined above. To begin with, Dan 7:2-8 describes four beasts emerging from the sea, a common Israelite image for chaos. The winged lion, reminiscent of the hybrid creatures guarding Mesopotamian palaces and temples (see Chapter 1), represents Babylonia, the bear stands for Media, and the leopard evokes Cyrus the Great's swift creation of an empire. The fourth beast is different, not being associated with any specific animal, because the Greeks from the west were different from any previous empire in Palestine, and its metallic nature and violent demeanor indicate the Greek army's aggressive military prowess. The ten horns are a round number to represent the Seleucid dynasty up until that time, the little horn is Antiochus IV, its arrogant words denote his decrees against Judaism and personal claims to divinity, while the three horns that are plucked are those who immediately preceded him: Seleucus IV, Heliodorus, who killed him, and Demetrius, Seleucus's son supplanted by Antiochus. Verses 23-24 explain that the beasts represent kingdoms and the horns represent kings, but unless one knows the political history of Alexander the Great's successors, there is nothing in the latter verses to indicate what kings or kingdoms are meant. Similarly verse 25 is understood only if one knows that

Antiochus IV spoke "against the Most High" and tried to do away with the Jewish festivals and the Torah. The chapter ends with the assurance that Antiochus will be judged and punished while the Jews will be vindicated (vv. 26-27).

Daniel 8 deals with some of the same events as well as some new ones. The shorter horn on the ram (v. 3) represents the Median Empire while the longer one represents the Persians, who come later and absorb the Medes. The Persians then expand their empire in all directions (v. 4). The goat from the west is Greece, and its great horn is Alexander the Great (v. 5). He overcomes the ram (the Persian Empire) quickly, but his empire is divided among four main successors upon his death (vv. 6-8). Verses 9-12 deal with Antiochus again, including his attacks on the Jews, his pride, and his elimination of sacrifice and disruption of the temple sanctuary while verse 13 adds a reference to the "transgression that makes desolate," indicating the altar to Zeus that Antiochus had erected in the temple and perhaps his image as well. Once again, the explanation of this imagery in human terms (vv. 23-25) does not provide any real insight without prior knowledge of the history of the time.

In Daniel 9, after Daniel prays for understanding concerning Jeremiah's prediction of a seventy-year exile, Gabriel comes to explain to Daniel that each year stands for seven years, such that they are now in the final seven-year period. The "anointed one" who is "cut off" (v. 26) is Onias III, who lost the high priesthood to Jason's bribe. The rest of the chapter describes Antiochus's actions yet again, including the "abomination that desolates," but promises that his end is "decreed" (v. 27). After fasting and prayer in Dan 10:2-9, Daniel receives another heavenly visitor, who in Chapter 11 describes a series of human interactions that, apart from the initial reference to Persia and Greece, is rather vague and general and does not specifically identify the individuals in question. But here, too, an awareness of the dealings between the Seleucids and the Ptolemies during the Third and Second Centuries B.C.E. is illuminating. For instance, the kings of the north and the south (v. 5) are those respective dynasties; the daughter of the southern king ratifying an agreement with the northern king followed by her loss of power alludes to the marriage of Berenice to Antiochus II in 253 B.C.E. and her murder in 246 B.C.E., which prompted Ptolemy III's invasion of Babylonia (vv. 6-9). Daniel 11:10-19 deal with the struggles between the two kingdoms for control of Palestine, while the enigmatic v. 20 alludes to Heliodorus's attempt to plunder the Temple treasury. Verses 21-39 cover Antiochus IV's military campaigns in Egypt and Judea, including being stopped by the Romans (the "Kittim" in v. 30). The final verses describe his last days; the fact that they are historically inaccurate indicates that they were written before the events they try to describe as an actual prediction. Chapter 12 assures Daniel of his people's ultimate vindication, introducing the concept of a bodily resurrection. By now an attentive reader will recognize the allusions to Antiochus in verses 7 and 11.

# CHAPTER 6

# Syro-Palestine

In addition to the large powers discussed in the previous chapters, Israel was surrounded by smaller nations and city-states often located even closer to home. Some of those discussed in this chapter predate the emergence of Israel and so had no direct interaction with it, but are included because their literary remains provide parallels to the biblical literature. After that I will consider Israel's historical contemporaries, with particular attention to their mutual involvement over time, along with relevant archaeological finds.

## Ebla

This city at the site of modern-day Tell Mardikh, fifty-three kilometers southwest of Aleppo in Syria, flourished circa 2600–2240 B.C.E., until it was destroyed by the Akkadian king Naram-sin. It had a resurgence under the Amorites (ca. 1800–1600 B.C.E.) but was then destroyed by the Hittites. It is most famous in biblical studies for the palace archives comprising close to twenty thousand texts, although many of them are fragments. These texts use the Sumerian script to write Eblaite, the second oldest recorded Semitic language (after Akkadian). Despite their number, however, they shed no significant new light on the biblical material,

85

other than to confirm the general makeup of the Semitic pantheon found closer in time to Israel at Ugarit, for instance, and reflected in some references within the First Testament itself (see further below under Ugarit). Thus we find references to Dagon, Ishtar (Ashtar), Resheph, Hadad (Ba'al), and Shapash. Some biblical names and locations have been identified in the Ebla texts, but in themselves they prove nothing about the historicity of the biblical texts written a millennium and more later. The most sensational claim, made soon after the texts were unearthed, was that the ending *-ya* in some names was a shortened form of Yahweh, the God of Israel. However, the cuneiform sign NI corresponds to *i-li*, meaning "my personal god," and since the divine name Ya is not found in any of the lists of gods or sacrifices at Ebla, any connection with Yahweh has long since been abandoned.

## Mari

The city of Mari was located at the site of the current Tell Hariri in the Syrian side of the Euphrates valley about two kilometers from the river and fifty kilometers north of the current Syrian-Iraq border. The city was founded near the beginning of the Third Millennium B.C.E. and prospered due to its strategic location on the route from Mesopotamia to Syria and westward to the Mediterranean and Egypt. It was destroyed in the middle of the Twenty-fourth Century B.C.E. by Sargon the Great, after which it persisted as a small village until it became an important Amorite city (ca. 1900 B.C.E.). This second period of vitality lasted until circa 1759 B.C.E., when the city was destroyed by Hammurabi of Babylon. After that, it was never more than a small village until it finally ceased to exist during Greek control of the region.

The most important period of Mari's history in terms of relevance to the First Testament is the second period of strength, and in particular the reign of Zimri-lim, its last king (ca. 1775-1761 B.C.E.). Approximately twenty thousand tablets dating mostly to his reign have been discovered, including administrative texts, diplomatic letters, and treaties, but the most significant for our purpose are about fifty texts that deal with one or another form of prophecy, which provide helpful background material for interpreting biblical prophets and prophecy. These texts consist of letters in which various royal officials from within the court as well as elsewhere report oracular utterances concerning the king that were spoken by different types of prophets. The most common topics are foreign affairs, especially victory in warfare, and warnings about dangers to the king's health or even his life, although there are also messages in which a particular deity calls upon the king to offer sacrifices to that god. The most common deities mentioned are Dagon and Ishtar, although one also finds Hadad, Shamash, and Marduk, among others.

The Mari texts reflect different types of prophets distinguished by their affiliations and by the terminology applied to them. Many of those who speak these prophetic messages are linked to a sanctuary (the *assinnu*), but more than half are laypeople with no such connections. The First Testament also reflects distinctions between professional prophets associated with the temple and others who are not. The most famous example of the latter is in Amos 7:10-14, when the priest Amaziah orders Amos to earn money by prophecy in Judah rather than at the sanctuary in Bethel, to which Amos retorts, "I am no prophet, nor a prophet's son [i.e., a member of a prophetic group]." Some Mari prophets operate alone while others appear as groups, to which we can compare the "band of prophets" (1 Sam 10:5, 10) and the "sons of the prophets" (1 Kings 20:35; 2 Kings 2:3, 5, 7, 15; 4:1, 38; 5:22; 9:1).

With respect to specific terminology, the most common term is *muḫḫûm/maḫḫutûm* (male and female, respectively), which derives from a verb meaning "to be crazy, to go into a frenzy." This suggests individuals who deliver their message while in a state of ecstasy, a phenomenon seen in the Bible as well. Balaam "falls down, but with eyes uncovered" (Num 24:4, 16), the prophets of Ba'al on Mount Carmel jump around and gash themselves (1 Kings 18:28-29), Saul twice falls in with groups of ecstatic prophets (1 Sam 10:5-13; 19:18-24), Elisha receives God's message while listening to music (2 Kings 3:15), Jeremiah speaks of God's word as a compulsion he cannot hold in (Jer 20:9) and compares himself to someone "overcome by wine" (Jer 23:9), and Ezekiel regularly describes himself as being overwhelmed by God's power, being lifted up by the hand of the Lord and physically transferred elsewhere in visions (e.g., Ezek 8:3). We can also compare this with the designation of prophets as "mad" (2 Kings 9:11; Jer 29:26; Hos 9:7).

The next most frequent classification includes the *āpilum/āpiltum* or "answerers," designating individuals who deliver a divine response to specific inquiries. Once again, this parallels an aspect of biblical prophecy. The first prophet, Samuel, is introduced as someone who can reveal the whereabouts of Saul's lost asses (1 Sam 9:5-10), David "inquired of the LORD" (2 Sam 5:19, 23, and elsewhere) about battle plans and received specific answers, "the king of Israel" and Jehoshaphat also sought messages from prophets prior to the battle at Ramoth-Gilead (1 Kings 22:6-15), Hezekiah consulted Isaiah during Sennacherib's siege of Jerusalem (2 Kings 19:2-7 // Isa 37:2-7), Josiah inquired of Huldah concerning the scroll that had been found in the temple (2 Kings 22:13-20), Zedekiah sent messengers to Jeremiah (Jer 21:1-7) and later spoke with him directly (Jer 37:3-10), and so on. Moreover, a prophetic message from Yahweh is often designated an "answer" (e.g., 1 Sam 9:17; Jer 23:37; Mic 3:7; 6:5).

Only one text refers to the *nabû*, a term cognate with *nābî'*, the Hebrew word for "prophet." The verb *nabû* means "to name, invoke," so the noun derived from it would mean "one who invokes (god[s])." In this lone text the *nabû* were specifically asked to obtain a message for the king, so they appear to function much like the *āpilum/āpiltum* in seeking a divine response, once again paralleling some biblical prophets and their activities.

Despite these similarities between prophecy at Mari and in the Bible, there are nonetheless differences. The first is in the area of content. The Mari texts are universally positive toward the king whereas biblical prophecy had both reassurance and condemnation, depending on the situation. Related to this is the fact that the Mari texts are all addressed to the king alone, but later biblical prophecy expanded its audience to encompass the people as a whole. This may be attributed to the fact that the Mari texts were all found in the palace and messages to others may have been preserved elsewhere, but in the absence of any evidence of more general addressees at Mari, the difference is striking. In addition, with the exception of one text that urges the king to hear the case of those who have been wronged, the Mari prophecies are devoid of the ethical content that runs throughout so much of biblical prophecy. Second, the status of oracular prophecy at Mari was decidedly lower than in the Bible. Many of the letters reporting divine messages were accompanied by a lock of the prophet's hair and/or material from the prophet's garment, presumably to be used in a more traditional divination ritual to test the veracity of the message. In contrast, although the biblical prophets and their messages were often rejected, the validity of the form in which the prophet received the message and delivered it to the audience was not questioned.

Although the Mari prophecies have attracted the most attention, other isolated texts are worth noting in relation to the First Testament. For example, texts from Mari describe how an agreement is ratified by cutting animals in half and walking between the parts. Similarly, in Gen 15:9-18, God establishes (literally, cuts) a covenant with Abraham when a smoking fire pot and a torch pass between the halves of animals that Abraham had cut up. The full significance of this ritual is made explicit in Jer 34:18-19, where Yahweh says that he will make those who broke the covenant like the calf they had cut in two and passed between. In other words, the ritual is meant to indicate the fate that awaits anyone who breaks the agreement being made. In addition, an Akkadian text describes Tiamat's defeat by the storm god of Aleppo, a motif that is much more developed at Ugarit in the battle between Ba'al and Sea and then between Yahweh and Sea in biblical texts (see further below). Finally, the moon god Sheger, also known from Ebla and Emar, is mentioned in Exod 13:12 and Deut 7:13; 28:4, 18, 51.

## Mitanni

Mitanni was a confederation of Hurrian states in northern Syria and Mesopotamia and southeast Anatolia (ca. 1550–1250 B.C.E.). It came together following the regional power vacuum created by the Hittite sack of Babylon in 1595 B.C.E., and by the beginning of the Fifteenth Century B.C.E. Mitanni had subjugated Assyria. Much of that century was spent battling Egypt for control of their border regions until a peace treaty was signed between the two countries and a royal marriage took place between the king's daughter and Pharaoh Thutmose IV around 1415 B.C.E. (see Chapter 2). This enabled Mitanni to focus on the Hittites, who were encroaching from the west, in some cases conquering Mitanni's vassals and in others encouraging their rebellion. Eventually, the Hittites began to attack Mitanni directly, and by the end of the Fourteenth Century B.C.E., Mitanni had become their vassal. Ashur-uballit I (1365–1330 B.C.E.) of Assyria took advantage of this to throw off Mitanni's shackles, and under the rule of Shalmaneser I (ca. 1273–1244 B.C.E.), Mitanni was reduced to an Assyrian province and lost its independence.

Mitanni is not mentioned in the Bible, since it ceased to exist prior to the latter's composition. The Hurrians are often equated with the Horites, mentioned in Gen 14:6; 36:20 and Deut 2:12, 22 as resident in Seir until displaced by the Edomites. However, this geographical location far to the south of known Hurrian territory, combined with the Semitic rather than Hurrian names of Horites in Gen 36:20-30, argues against this correlation (see further below under Edom).

Notwithstanding this lack of direct connection, texts from the Hurrian city of Nuzi near the Tigris River (thirteen kilometers southwest of modern Kirkuk in northern Iraq) are frequently proposed as providing background for some practices in the patriarchal narratives. For instance, at Nuzi slaves or servants were sometimes adopted when a couple had no heir, just as Abraham designated his slave Eliezer to be his heir (Gen 15:2-3). Later, Abraham's barren wife, Sarah, provides him with her servant girl Hagar to bear him children, but when Sarah gives birth to Isaac, he becomes the heir (Gen 16; 21:1-21), and the Nuzi tablets regulate similar situations where a wife bears children to her husband after a servant girl has already done so. In Genesis 24, Laban arranges the marriage of his sister to Isaac through Abraham's messenger and seeks her consent (v. 58), but when it comes to marrying his own daughters to Jacob, he does not consult them (Genesis 29). This matches the practice at Nuzi, where marriage contracts include a sister's agreement to the marriage, but not a daughter's.

Wills from Nuzi have some bearing on the issue of levirate marriage (Deut 25:5-10; cf. Genesis 38; Ruth 4), in which a widow who has not borne children to her deceased husband may marry only her husband's brother, and the firstborn of the second union will be considered the deceased brother's heir. The purpose is clearly to keep property from transferring outside the family, and a similar concern is evident in four Nuzi wills: if a widow wishes to remarry, she must first be stripped naked before leaving the house. In addition to the humiliation involved, this ritual act entails symbolic renunciation of her claim to any property, thus ensuring that it remains within the original household, just as in the case of levirate marriage. Granted, Deut 25:5 absolutely prohibits such marriage outside the husband's family, but the principle remains nonetheless. These texts also illuminate Hos 2:2-3, in which the prophet threatens to strip his adulterous wife. In light of the Nuzi texts, the point is not only to humiliate the woman but also to indicate her lack of financial support.

Also in terms of inheritance, the legal validity of deathbed blessings at Nuzi is relevant for those of Isaac over Jacob and Esau (Genesis 27), Jacob over his and Joseph's sons (Genesis 48–49), and Moses over Israel (Deuteronomy 33). Similarly, the jealousy that Joseph's brothers display toward him may reflect a concern that their father might designate him as the heir despite his birth order, just as could be done at Nuzi.

Another Nuzi legal text is often cited in terms of inheritance in relationship to the episode in Genesis 31: Rachel takes the *teraphim* ("household gods," v. 19) when she and Jacob leave her father Laban's house to return to Canaan, and when Laban catches up with them, he asks about his "gods" (v. 30; cf. v. 32). In the Nuzi text, an individual named Nashwi adopts Wullu and marries him to his daughter. The text specifies that if Nashwi subsequently has a son of his own, he and Wullu are to split the property, but the household gods pass to the natural-born son alone. However, if there is no subsequent birth, Wullu will inherit the gods as well. In light of this, the Genesis 31 story has been interpreted in terms of Rachel seeking to retain some claim to inheritance, either on her own or in the name of Jacob, but neither of them would have any claim to do so, since Laban had legitimate sons. Moreover, the analogy is not exact, since in the Nuzi text, Wullu still inherits half the property even without possessing the family gods. Rather, the transfer of the family gods indicates who carries on the family line, which explains Laban's intense desire to retrieve them. In

91

contrast, another Nuzi document contains a son's complaint that his mother gave the family gods to another man, perhaps her second husband, in which case Rachel may simply have wished to retain a connection to the family she was leaving behind as she and Jacob traveled back to Canaan. This is supported by the association of the Nuzi household gods with "the dead" in three texts, two of which deal with individuals being disinherited and the third concerned with an inheritor. This indicates a connection between the Nuzi household gods and ancestor worship, which reinforces the important role both they and the *teraphim* played with respect to family continuity and solidarity.

One final alleged parallel must be noted, specifically because it has not withstood closer scrutiny. Abraham twice tells foreign rulers that his wife, Sarah, is his sister (Gen 12:10-20; 20:1-18), and his son Isaac does the same thing (Gen 26:1-11). Such a violation of the marriage laws against incest (Lev 18:9, 11; 20:17; Deut 27:22) has been explained by appeal to Nuzi texts in which a man could supposedly adopt his wife in order to give her higher legal status. However, the texts used to support this claim actually deal with a man adopting a woman as his sister and agreeing to find her someone else as a husband. In one text the first man subsequently marries the woman, requiring a separate contract, but the sequence is the opposite from that presupposed for the patriarchal stories. The closest possible parallel to the patriarchs' claim is in the last text above, wherein a male is adopted by a woman's father, thus becoming her brother, and subsequently marrying her, but this is not really the same case as in the three biblical passages either. Genesis 20:12 solves the supposed moral problem by asserting that Sarah is Abraham's half sister, even though this is not mentioned at any point in the preceding narratives, but the fact remains that the Nuzi texts do not help explain away the patriarchs' claims about their wives.

Despite this last example, these parallels between some Nuzi documents of the Second Millennium B.C.E. and the patriarchal narratives were once cited as proof of the historicity of the patriarchal narratives and even their date of composition. However, subsequent research has demonstrated that comparable customs can also be found in first-millennium texts from the ancient Near East, which means they could just have easily been composed later.

Nevertheless, the Nuzi texts help clarify many of the customs and family practices found in the stories of Israel's ancestors.

# Emar

Emar occupied the site of contemporary Tell Meskene, on the banks of the Euphrates about one hundred kilometers southeast of Aleppo. The city was subject to the king of Carchemish, representing Hittite authority in the region. Despite references to Emar from Ebla (ca. 2900 B.C.E.) and Mari (ca. 1800 B.C.E.), the current site dates no earlier than the end of the Fourteenth Century B.C.E. This anomaly is due to changes in the path of the Euphrates necessitating that the city be moved. The modern salvage excavations at the site were required by impending flooding of the areas due to the construction of the Tabqa Dam and resulted in more than one thousand texts dated from the new city's origins until its destruction in 1187 B.C.E. Some of these are relevant for the meaning of the Hebrew word for "prophet," plus some customs and selected biblical texts.

The Hebrew word for a "prophet" (*nabî*) has traditionally been interpreted as the passive of the Akkadian verb *nabû*, "to call," resulting in the meaning "one who is called" by god. However, we saw above that the *nabû* in Ebla derived their title from the meaning "to name, invoke," suggesting the nuance of "one who invokes" the gods. Emar also yields a reference to the *na-bi-i* in connection with the goddess Ishhara, as well as four instances of the female *munabbiātu* linked to the same deity. In the only two instances at Emar of the verb *nabû*, from which these terms are derived, an heiress is called to "invoke" the family deities. Such initiative on the part of an individual, as opposed to being the passive object of divine inspiration, is reflected in two biblical texts. In 1 Kings 18:24, Elijah challenges the prophets of Ba'al to "call on the name of your god and I will call on the name of the LORD," and whichever deity sends fire from heaven will be the true God over Israel. Similarly, when the Syrian commander Naaman approaches Elisha to be healed, he is disappointed that the prophet simply tells him to wash in the Jordan River rather than "call on the name of the LORD" (2 Kings 5:11).

Emar texts also relate to two biblical matters already noted at Nuzi, namely, the *teraphim* and the levirate marriage. In two Emar wills, an individual designates his daughter as both female and male; this legal fiction is probably so that she is eligible to inherit his property. In both wills, this is followed by the stipulation that she is to call upon "my gods and my dead." The latter refers to the deceased ancestors and the former to the household gods, parallel to the biblical *teraphim*. As at Nuzi, these texts show a connection between the household gods (and by extension the *teraphim*) with the continuation of a father's household, which in turn is relevant for a fuller understanding of the episode in Genesis 31. In addition, two Emar texts duplicate the procedure at Nuzi for a widow who wishes to remarry, namely, that she first strip naked and leave her clothes in the house. Significantly, both the Emar texts and Deut 25:5 specify that this occurs when the widow wishes to marry a "stranger" (literally, "a strange man"); this cognate terminology (in Akkadian and Hebrew) reinforces the relevance of the Emar text for understanding better the retention of family property through levirate marriage in the biblical material. As with the Nuzi texts, these two Emar wills also shed light on the prophet stripping his wife before expelling her (Hos 2:2-3). Together, these parallels show that both concepts reflected in these different texts were not restricted to a single location in the ancient Near East.

# Ugarit

Ugarit was the capital of a small but significant kingdom in northern Syria during the Second Millennium B.C.E. Located at modern-day Ras Shamra, Ugarit controlled a territory of about two thousand square kilometers, ranging from Jebel el-Aqra in the north to Jable in the south and from the Mediterranean to the Alaouite Mountains in the east. Its importance is due in large part to its port, modern-day Minet el-Beida, which facilitated trade between Mediterranean states and Mesopotamia. During the course of its history, Ugarit came under the influence of the Egyptians, then the Hurrians of Mitanni, the Egyptians once again, and finally the Hittites, until it was destroyed circa 1180 B.C.E. by the Sea Peoples.

Ugarit's significance for biblical scholars is rooted in the collection of texts found there, both in terms of the language used and their content. Excavators have found different collections of clay tablets inscribed with cuneiform writing, comprising letters, administrative texts, and religious literature. The Ugaritic cuneiform language was alphabetic, representing a total of thirty letters, unlike the syllabic cuneiform of ancient Sumerian and Akkadian (and its offshoots, Babylonian and Assyrian), which required hundreds of signs to represent all possible combinations of consonants and vowels. While there is general agreement that Ugaritic is part of the Northwest Semitic group of languages, as is Hebrew, scholars disagree whether Ugaritic is a precursor to Hebrew or whether they represent different branches of a linguistic tree. In either case, Ugaritic has proved helpful for understanding biblical Hebrew in terms of both grammar and vocabulary.

In terms of grammar, two examples will show how knowledge of Ugaritic can change our understanding of biblical texts. Translated literally, Ps 73:1 reads, "Surely good to Israel [is] God to the pure of heart"; the repeated "to" makes the line awkward, and many commentators divide the Hebrew for "to Israel" (*lyśr'l*) in order to yield, "Surely good to the upright [is] God (*lyśr 'l*), God to the pure of heart." However, in Ugaritic the preposition translated here as "to" can also indicate the vocative (direct address), which provides a more intelligible translation without altering the Hebrew text, namely, "Surely good, O Israel, is God to the pure of heart." An Ugaritic preposition with two meanings also sheds light on Prov 25:21-22, which urges giving enemies food or drink so that, according to the NRSV translation, "you will heap coals of fire on their heads." This is usually interpreted to mean that their anger will increase so much that they will recognize that their attitude is too extreme and repent. However, the verb translated "heap" really means "snatch, take away," which is not consistent with the preposition translated as "on." But in Ugaritic that preposition can also mean "from," which would result in "you will snatch burning coals *from* their heads." In that case, the verse means that acts of kindness will take away the heat of an enemy's anger, which makes more sense.

Ugaritic can also clarify biblical texts in terms of vocabulary. Sometimes a word that occurs only once or twice in the First

Testament is found much more frequently in the Ugaritian literature, and by taking into account the more numerous contexts for
the latter, especially if they include parallel terms in poetic literature, we can gain a better understanding of the rarer Hebrew
word. For instance, Amos 1:1 says that the prophet was a *nqd*,
which is usually translated as "shepherd," even though it is not
the usual Hebrew word for "shepherd." The word *nqd* occurs only
one other time in the First Testament, at 2 Kings 3:4, where it is
used of King Mesha of Moab. This suggests it does not mean a
solitary rustic pastoral herder, an unusual designation for a king,
but the exact nuance is not obvious. However, the term *nqd* occurs
a number of times in the Ugaritian literature, where it indicates
royal servants who could be called upon for military service.
Thus, in the Ugaritian texts the *nqd* held positions of importance
and influence. Rather than simple shepherds, they managed large
herds. In addition to being more consistent with King Mesha, this
understanding of the term would explain Amos's presence in the
north, probably to sell his product, despite his home at Tekoa in
the south, as well as his knowledge not only of northern affairs
but also of those in the surrounding countries (see Amos 1–2).

Ugaritic vocabulary can also provide a new understanding for
Judg 5:17b, which asks, "Dan, why did he abide with the ships?"
rather than go to the battle when Deborah summoned them.
While the line is perfectly understandable in itself, Dan's tribal territory was well inland from the Mediterranean, which raises questions about the correctness of the word translated as "ships."
However, three Ugarit texts contain the word *'an*/*'any* (ease),
whose consonants are comparable to the Hebrew *'nywt* (ships),
and in one instance the Ugaritic word is the object of the verb *gr*, a
cognate to the Hebrew verb *gwr* used in Judg 5:17b. Reading the
biblical text in light of the Ugaritic term yields, "Dan, why did he
remain at ease?" which eliminates the problem of their geographical location. Another instance where Ugaritic can help with an
apparent geographical difficulty is found in Ps 48:3 (Eng v. 2),
which says that Mount Zion is "in the far north," even though it is
actually in Jerusalem, in southern Israel (see also its association
with Judah in v. 12 [Eng. v. 11]). Hebrew and Ugaritic use the
same word for "north," namely, *ṣāpôn*/*ṣpn*, but in Ugaritic it is
derived from Mount Zaphon (Jebel el-Aqra), north of Ugarit and

the highest mountain in Syria, which was considered the home of the storm god Baʿal. In this light, the term in Ps 48:3 (Eng v. 2) is not meant to indicate Zion's physical location but identifies it as a mythological holy mountain.

Even more than such individual points of grammar and vocabulary, the content of the Ugarit texts sheds light on the biblical material. While the various letters and administrative texts provide some general background for the cultural and political context of the period, in relation to the Bible, scholarly attention has focused on the religious texts from Ugarit as a means of reconstructing Canaanite religion. Prior to the discovery of the Ugarit texts, the primary source of information for Canaanite religion was the First Testament, which provided a decidedly negative evaluation of it, plus occasional references in ancient authors writing many centuries later. The Ugarit texts appear to provide us with Canaanite religious texts written by actual practitioners of the religion, leading some to nickname those texts the "Canaanite Bible." However, the Ugarit texts must be used with a degree of caution since there are chronological and physical distances between Ugarit and the Canaanites in the Bible. As mentioned above, Ugarit was destroyed circa 1180 B.C.E., shortly after Israel began to establish itself in the land. Moreover, Ugarit is well to the north of "biblical" Canaan, but it does fall within the geographic boundaries of Canaan as understood by the Egyptians. Without insisting on an exact correlation between Ugaritian and Canaanite religion, the religious texts from Ugarit parallel what we know of Canaanite religion from the Bible and other ancient sources and can help us gain a fuller picture of that religion. Those texts also demonstrate the degree to which Israelite religion paralleled Canaanite religion, including the ways in which the presentation of Yahweh adopts but also adapts elements from the Canaanite gods.

The Ugarit religious texts can be categorized as either ritual or mythology. The former includes references to various types of sacrifices and offerings as well as different cultic personnel. In most cases the terms used are identical to those used for sacrifices, offerings, and personnel in biblical texts, indicating common practices and a similar temple bureaucracy. Included among the latter at Ugarit are male "holy/dedicated ones" (qdšm), using a term that occurs in both masculine and feminine forms in the First Testament, where they have been understood as cultic prostitutes who reenacted the fertility cult. However, the term has no such association at Ugarit, where it simply refers to minor temple functionaries without any indication of sexual activity on their part. This has led some scholars to challenge the idea that fertility rituals were a rampant element of Israelite religion borrowed from the Canaanites. Granted, the term for a female "holy/dedicated one" always occurs in parallel with the Hebrew word for "prostitute" (Gen 38:15, 21-22, 24; Deut 23:18-19 [Eng vv. 17-18]; Hos 4:14), but only Deut 23:18-19 includes a general reference to the Temple. With respect to the term for males, it is parallel to "prostitute" only in Deut 23:18-19, but not in the other four occurrences of the term (1 Kings 14:24; 15:12; 22:47 [Eng v. 46]; 2 Kings 23:7), and only Deut 23:18-19 and 2 Kings 23:7 link the males to the Temple. Furthermore, neither term occurs in connection with fertility rituals. Thus, although Deuteronomy and Kings have a decidedly negative view of them, especially the men, there is nothing to indicate it had anything to do with supposed Canaanite fertility rituals, which are not reflected in any Ugarit ritual texts either, whether they mention the *qdšm* or not.

In the Ugarit mythological texts we find stories about the deities of Ugarit, which provide additional details concerning deities with the same names in the Bible as well. The head of the Ugarit pantheon is El, who is usually depicted as an old, bearded man. The texts identify him as the creator and father of the gods (and of humans) who dwells in a large tent and is seated upon a cherubim throne, on a holy mountain in the far north at the source of the waters. He is frequently characterized as kind, caring, healing, and wise. The general parallels with Yahweh are obvious, especially Yahweh's abode in a tent sanctuary prior to the construction of the Temple as well as his cherubim throne in both types of sanctuaries. Moreover, specific texts dealing with Yahweh seem to draw upon El traditions, most notably Dan 7:9 where a white-haired deity is enthroned in heaven. This reflects the Ugarit descriptions of El as an old man, and the title "Ancient One" (literally, "Ancient of Days," Dan 7:9, 13) echoes El's epithet, "Father of Years." These points of contact between the two deities indicate that El and Yahweh were assimilated, and based on the lack of polemic against El (contrast below concerning Baʿal) in the First Testament, this probably happened at a very early stage of Israelite religion. Nevertheless, traces of the god El can still be found in the First Testament, although detecting them is difficult because the Hebrew word ʾ*ēl* can mean either the deity El or simply the noun "god." Deciding which meaning applies in different texts requires attention to the context as well as information from the Ugarit texts.

One place the god El might be found is in texts where ʾ*ēl* is followed by an epithet or title. Five of these occur only once each: Gen 14:18-22 mentions ʾ*ēl* ʿ*elyôn* (God/El Most High), Gen 16:13 refers to ʾ*ēl* *rōʾi* (God/El Sees), ʾ*ēl* ʿ*ôlām* (God/El Eternal) is named in Gen 21:33, Gen 35:7 contains ʾ*ēl* *bêt-*ʾ*ēl* (God/El of Bethel), and ʾ*ēl* *bĕrît* (God/El of the covenant) is found in Judg 9:46. There is nothing specifically characteristic of the god El in the second phrase, but the epithets in Gen 14:18-22; 21:33 reflect traditions associated with El at Ugarit (and elsewhere). The word ʿ*elyôn* (most high) was applied to various gods in the ancient world, including El in some inscriptions, and it is certainly an appropriate title for the high god of the Canaanite pantheon as well. Moreover, in Gen 14:19 the deity is also called "maker of heaven and earth," which is an expansion of "El, creator/maker of the earth" found in many inscriptions as well as the divine name Elkunirša in a Hittite myth discovered at Bogazköy but clearly reflecting Semitic traditions about El, Baʿal, and Asherah (see Chapter 3). In light of these associations between El and Elyon, the references to ʾ*ēl* ʿ*elyôn* in Gen 14:18-22 probably refer to El rather than the more general "God." By extension, references to Elyon alone may also refer to the Canaanite deity rather than to Yahweh; however, each instance would need to be evaluated individually, a task beyond the scope of this work.

A similar case can be made with respect to ʾ*ēl* ʿ*ôlām* (God/El Eternal); ʿ*ôlām* is applied to El at Ugarit as well as in other ancient inscriptions. In addition, El is described as old and wise in a number of Ugaritic texts and, as noted above, is called "the Father of Years" there. This supports taking "the Eternal (One)" here as a title for El as well. This in turn has implications for translating Ps 75:10 (Eng v. 9), where ʿ*ôlām* is paralleled in the next line by "the God of Jacob"; rather than translate the first line as "I will rejoice

99

forever," rendering it instead as "I will rejoice for the Eternal One" makes a better parallel to "I will sing praises to the God of Jacob" in the second line.

This leaves us with the phrases in Gen 16:13; 35:7; and Judg 9:46. As noted before, seeing is too common and general an attribute to be linked solely to El. Similarly, Gen 35:7 could mean simply "the god of Bethel," although the evidence adduced below for El as the god of the patriarchs, especially Jacob, supports rendering it as "El of Bethel." Similarly, *'ēl běrît* in Judg 9:46 is mentioned at Shechem, which recalls Jacob's dedication of an altar there to El (Gen 33:20; see further below), and *ba'al běrît* (lord of the covenant) in Judg 8:33; 9:4 is probably an epithet of El. If so, Judg 9:46 would be a shortened form of "El, Lord of the covenant."

A more frequent *'ēl* + epithet formulation is *'ēl šadday*, which occurs eight times in the First Testament, while the two words are split across adjoining lines of parallel poetry another thirteen times. The biblical El Shaddai is traditionally rendered as "God Almighty" under the influence of the Greek translation as *pantokratōr* and the Latin *omnipotens*, but *šadday* is better explained as a plural, meaning "mountains." While this might simply mean the general "God of the mountains," the translation "El of the mountains" fits the common Ugaritic description of El's residence on the cosmic mountain(s) and his explicit designation in one Ugarit text as "El, the one of the mountain" (cf. "the mountains of El/God," Ps 36:7 [Eng v. 6]); "mighty mountains" in the NRSV). Moreover, the phrase "El Shaddai" occurs at Ugarit, as well as in at least one other ancient inscription, while in the Bible, Shaddai is paralleled with Elyon, an El title as we have seen, in Num 24:16 and Ps 91:1. The fact that Shaddai was considered an ancient divine name is evident in that thirty-one of the forty-one occurrences of Shaddai by itself are found in the deliberately archaizing book of Job, where with one exception (Job 12:9, which is probably an addition), Job and his friends never refer to God as Yahweh.

Even more striking than these El epithets are two instances in the First Testament where the word *'ēl* is followed immediately by *'ělōhîm*, which is the more common Hebrew noun meaning "god." Most Bibles translate the name that Jacob gives to a site near Shechem as "God, the God of Israel" (Gen 33:20) and the divine address to Jacob in Gen 46:3 as "God, the God of your father."

Although these are possible literal translations of the Hebrew, there is no reason to use two different words for "God" immediately next to each other. It makes more sense to take the first word as the name of the deity and translate these two verses as "El, the God of Israel" and "El, the God of your father," in which case these two verses indicate that El was the original name of the deity worshiped by the group(s) who preserved these stories. This is reinforced by an allusion to El in Gen 49:24. The second line refers to blessings from what is usually translated as "the Mighty One of Jacob," but the Hebrew word translated as "Mighty One" contains the exact consonants as the word for "bull." "The Bull" was another title for El in the Ugarit texts, and since early Hebrew wrote only the consonants, either "mighty one" or "bull" is a possible translation since they look the same without the vowels. However, the cluster of El titles in the next verse supports taking it as bull: Gen 49:25 speaks of "blessings by El, your father" (not "God *of* your father"; see "the blessings of your father," v. 26) and by Shaddai. Moreover, "the blessings of the breasts and of the womb" (v. 25) allude to the fertility associations of Asherah, El's wife, yet more evidence of an Ugarit background to this passage.

In sum, the chief Canaanite god is present in a number of biblical texts dealing with the patriarchs and matriarchs. Eventually, as El and Yahweh came to be seen as a single deity, Yahweh in turn became equated with these early texts. For instance, in Exod 3:6 he says that Moses' ancestors knew him as "the God of your father, the God of Abraham, the God of Isaac, and the God of Jacob," and Exod 6:3 states that they knew him as El Shaddai. Similarly, all other instances explicitly identify "the bull of Jacob" as Yahweh (see Isa 49:26; 60:16; Ps 132:2, 5; and "the bull of Israel," Isa 1:24). With time, these associations with the El were lost to memory, leading to 'el being understood as the generic noun "god" and the vowels for "mighty one" being inserted into the consonants for "bull." Knowledge of the Ugarit texts allows us to reconstruct this early stage of Israelite religion.

El's wife at Ugarit was Athirat, which corresponds to the Hebrew Asherah. Athirat was called "the mother of the gods" (she is said to have seventy sons) and was associated with fertility. In keeping with this, she is often depicted as a tree or as a naked woman with exaggerated breasts and pubic area. The Hebrew term *ʾăšērâ* occurs forty times in the First Testament, usually accompanied by a verb indicating human construction, such as *make, build,* or *erect.* Other verbs such as *cut* and *burn* suggest that it was made of wood, and thus most modern translations translate it as "sacred pole" or something similar, and based on the goddess Asherah's association with trees, many scholars think it was carved in the shape of a tree. However, this object's connection with a goddess of the same name was only clearly recognized after the Ugarit texts were discovered. In light of the prominent role of the goddess Asherah there, scholars now recognize that at least five instances of the term in the First Testament refer to a deity and not an object. Judges 3:7 mentions plural "Asherahs" in parallel with "the Baʿals"; there the two terms have the sense of "goddesses" and "gods" in general. More specifically, in 1 Kings 15:13 Asa removes his mother from her role as queen mother "because she had made an abominable image for Asherah," 2 Kings 21:7 notes that Manasseh made a "carved image of Asherah," and 2 Kings 23:4 mentions vessels made for Asherah (among others). But one does not make vessels for—or of—another object, and more important, people make images of deities, not cultic items. First Kings 18:19 refers to the prophets of Asherah, and prophets dedicated to an object rather than a god or goddess would be unprecedented in the ancient Near East. Thus, it is now generally accepted that the asherah poles were sacred items linked to the cult of a goddess with the same name, Asherah.

It is clear that Asherah and her cultic item were prevalent throughout ancient Israel. The Deuteronomistic History frequently claims that the Israelites set up asherah poles "on every high hill and under every green tree" (e.g., 2 Kings 17:10). Large numbers of figurines depicting a naked woman holding her breasts have been found throughout Judah, including in Jerusalem, and their association with Asherah supports the biblical claim concerning the extent to which she was worshiped. In fact, Asherah and her symbol were even connected to the worship of Yahweh. Deut 16:21 declares, "You shall not plant any tree as [an asherah] beside the altar of Yahweh," and since legislators do not typically enact regulations against actions that are not occurring, this verse indicates that Asherah was actively worshiped in Israel—even in Yahweh's temple in Jerusalem. This is confirmed by 2 Kings 21:7, which states that King Manasseh placed "the carved image of Asherah" in the temple. Archaeological discoveries have also linked Yahweh and Asherah. Two inscriptions dating to circa 800 B.C.E. from Kuntillet Ajrûd, an ancient rest stop in the northern Sinai peninsula about eighty kilometers south of Kadesh-Barnea, read in part, "I bless you by YHWH of Samaria [or Teman] and by his asherah." A similar formula invoking Yahweh and "his asherah" was found in a grave inscription from the mid-Eighth Century B.C.E. at Khirbet-el-Qom in central Judah. The possessive pronoun *his* means *asherah* cannot be the name of the goddess but must be an object linked to Yahweh; however, it makes the most sense to associate it with the goddess as well, thereby establishing a connection between the deities Yahweh and Asherah. Similarly, an Israelite cult stand from the Tenth Century B.C.E. depicts Asherah on two levels, as a tree and then a naked woman, both flanked by lions. The other two levels contain a sun disc and an empty space, both of which have been taken to indicate Yahweh, especially the lack of an image (the empty space) on level three (cf. the prohibition of images in Exod 20:4).

The Deuteronomistic History presents a negative evaluation of Asherah and her symbol, but this view was not universally held in ancient Israel. There is no opposition to her among the early prophets: such strong Yahwists as Elijah and Elisha never speak against her or the object, and if the reference to her prophets in 1 Kings 18:19 is authentic, it is even more striking that at the end of the chapter Ba'al's prophets are killed while hers are left untouched. Similarly, after Jehu's purge of Ba'al's priests from Samaria, Elihu pronounces in God's name, "You have done well in carrying out what [is right in my eyes]" (2 Kings 10:30). But 2 Kings 13:6 states that during the reign of Jehu's son Jehoahaz, "the sacred pole . . . *remained* in Samaria" (emphasis mine), which means it had been there earlier during Jehu's religious purge. The absence of a rebuke by Elisha over this suggests that both he and Jehu considered the asherah pole acceptable. In the same way, none of the Eighth-Century prophets (Isaiah, Amos, Hosea, and Micah) voiced any opposition to Asherah or her symbol. In light of Hosea's strong opposition to "pagan" elements such as Ba'al, standing stones, and high places, his silence concerning Asherah stands in stark relief. In fact, the word occurs only four times in the entire prophetic corpus (Isa 17:7-8; 27:9; Jer 17:2; Mic 5:13 [Eng v. 14]), and these come from shortly before the Babylonian exile or later. The logical conclusion is that some Israelites began to consider Asherah incompatible with Yahweh only at that later stage in the nation's history.

Another major Ugaritic deity is Baʿal, the storm god, whose name means "lord." He is depicted on a stele brandishing a war club in one hand and a lance ending in a jagged form representing lightning in his other hand. A large portion of the Ugarit mythological texts deals with his battles to establish and then maintain his kingship. First, he defeats Yam (Sea), using two clubs symbolizing thunder and lightning, after which he is proclaimed king. The text then describes the construction of Baʿal's palace, followed by Mot (Death) taking Baʿal into the underworld, which reflects the absence of rain during the summer months in the region. Baʿal's sister Anat follows them, kills Mot, and brings Baʿal back, restoring the rains during the winter months, and Baʿal resumes his throne.

There is no doubt that Baʿal is reflected in the First Testament: the references to Israelites worshiping him are too numerous even to list, let alone discuss. It is clear, however, that this generated intense opposition at an early stage. Unlike El, who is not subject to negative polemic in the biblical texts, Baʿal is, usually by the same people who accepted Asherah. Rather, Baʿal was seen as a clear threat to Yahweh's supremacy that must be opposed. This was linked to the issue of fertility, a central matter in Israel where agriculture was so dependent on the winter rains in order to survive the dry summer period. Thus, while Elijah's conflict with the four hundred prophets of Baʿal on Mount Carmel (1 Kings 18) is probably against Melqart, the "Baʿal" of Tyre (see below), the concern with who was responsible for the rain in Israel, and therefore the fertility, reflects the Ugaritian Baʿal tradition as well. In the midst of a three-year drought (v. 1), Elijah proposes that whichever god is truly responsible for fertility demonstrate this by sending fire from heaven (vv. 24, 38), that is, lightning that accompanies storm clouds. When Yahweh does so after Baʿal has failed, the Lord's supremacy is established. In the same way, Hosea's argument with the people of Israel is that they have mistaken Baʿal as the source of fertility when it is in fact Yahweh.

But despite this rejection of Baʿal himself, Yahweh takes on some of Baʿal's characteristics as a way of negating Baʿal's appeal: if what Baʿal offers is already found in and through Yahweh, there is less reason to turn away from Yahweh. The most obvious and general parallel is the characterization of both as storm gods, although this almost certainly predates the encounter with Baʿal and his worshipers. For instance, the theophany at Sinai, when Yahweh is manifested in thunder from the clouds on the mountaintop, shows that Yahweh was already understood in those terms during the Exodus and Wilderness narratives. Nevertheless, the biblical presentation at times reflects that aspect of Baʿal as found in the Ugarit texts. Psalm 29 is a good example. The poem describes Yahweh being manifested in thunder and lightning, but beyond this general portrait, it also reflects themes from the Baʿal cycle at Ugarit, including domination over the Sea (vv. 3, 10) and divine kingship (v. 10). Moreover, the psalm mentions thunder (Yahweh's voice) seven times (vv. 3, 4 [twice], 5, 7, 8, 9), echoing an Ugarit text referring to Baʿal's seven lightnings and eight thunders as he sits enthroned "like the flood." Some have gone so far as to suggest that this was originally a Canaanite poem, with Yahweh's name being substituted for Baʿal's, but the reference to the wilderness (v. 8) demonstrates its Israelite origins, without denying that the author may have directly drawn on Baʿal imagery.

In keeping with the storm imagery, there is also a parallel between Yahweh and Baʿal in terms of their movement through the air. One of Baʿal's common titles in the Ugarit texts is "the rider on the clouds," which is often compared with Ps 68:5 (Eng v. 4). However, contrary to the NRSV's "him who rides upon the clouds," the latter actually says "the one who rides in the deserts," which fits the references to Yahweh coming from Sinai in verses 9 and 18 (Eng vv. 8, 17). Nonetheless, the rain in verse 9 (Eng v. 8) presumes the presence of clouds, and since the difference between the Hebrew words for "clouds" and "deserts" is just one consonant, the psalmist may still have had Baʿal's title in mind. Moreover, Yahweh does fly through the air, often in conjunction with clouds (Deut 33:26; Pss 18:10-12 [Eng vv. 9-11]; 68:34 [Eng v. 33], note "the rider"; 104:3; Isa 19:1 [again, "rider" appears]; Jer 4:13; Nah 1:3). This culminates in the one like a human being who comes "with the clouds of heaven" (Dan 7:13). Just as the Ancient One draws upon El imagery, this figure used Ba'al traditions, but as mediated through Israelite Yahwism.

Another point of contact between Ba'al and Yahweh lies in the former's battle with and defeat of Sea (Yam). Yahweh is sometimes described battling against the waters in connection with the creation of the world (Pss 74:12-17; 89:10-13 [Eng vv. 9-12]); the first text links this with Yahweh's kingship, as with Ba'al at Ugarit, a connection we have already seen at Ps 29:3, 10 and made as well in Psalm 93. Linked to this is the figure of Leviathan, mentioned in Ps 74:14 and elsewhere, who duplicates a sea monster named Litanu (sometimes spelled as Lotan) that was defeated by Ba'al or by Anat according to a second text. The Ugarit texts refer to him as a "fleeing," "twisting," and "crooked" serpent with seven heads. The last element clarifies Leviathan's plural "heads" (Ps 74:14), while Job's reference to Yahweh's piercing "the fleeing serpent" (Job 26:13) alludes to these texts as well, especially in light of Sea and Rahab, another sea monster, in Job 26:12 (see also God's treatment of Rahab in Job 9:13; Ps 89:11 [Eng v. 10]). A reference to Litanu is explicit in Isa 27:1, where Leviathan is called "the fleeing serpent . . . the twisting serpent" as well as a dragon. The identification of Leviathan as a dragon in turn allows us to recognize Ba'al's battle with the forces of the sea as the background to the dragons in Ps 74:13 (with Leviathan named, v. 14) and Job 7:12 (linked to Sea). The Exodus is expressed in terms of Yahweh's victory over Rahab, the dragon, in Isa 51:9-10 while Pss 77:17-21 (Eng vv. 16-20); 106:9; 114:3, 5 all use the same motif of defeating the waters without using the names. Egypt is also called Rahab (Ps 87:4; Isa 30:7) while Pharaoh is called a dragon (Ezek 29:3; 32:2), as is the king of Babylon (Jer 51:34). Yahweh's defeat of unnamed invaders is also described in terms of a battle against the waters (Hab 3:8, 10, 15).

The association between Leviathan and the dragon is also relevant to the description of Leviathan alongside Behemoth in Job 40–41. Many explain them as the crocodile and the hippopotamus, respectively, but unlike a crocodile, Leviathan breathes fire and smoke like a dragon (Job 41:18-21), which helps explain why humans cannot control him and therefore live in terror of him. This is a mythological creature that Yahweh can subdue, but Job cannot. The negative effect that Leviathan would have if unleashed, therefore, underlies Job's invocation of "those who are skilled to rouse up Leviathan" (once again paralleled with Sea) in 3:8 as part of his curse aiming to return creation to a state of chaos and darkness. We can note how the mythological background to all these texts is highlighted when they are compared with others where Yahweh simply *controls* the waters at the creation of the world rather than fights them (Gen 1:2, 6-10; Job 38:8-11; Pss 33:7; 104:5-9; Prov 8:27-29; Jer 5:22).

On the other hand, Baʿal's conflict with the god Death (Mot) at Ugarit is not reflected in the First Testament, although one episode during Baʿal's period in the underworld seems to lie behind the poem about the "son of Dawn" who seeks to make his throne "on the heights of Zaphon" but is brought down to the underworld (Isa 14:12-15). At Ugarit, Athtar, who is associated with the morning star (Venus), seeks to replace Baʿal, but when he climbs onto Baʿal's throne on Mount Zaphon, Athtar's legs do not reach the ground, and he is forced to withdraw in disgrace. On the other hand, Death as a deity is reflected in the First Testament. Isaiah 28:15, 18 refers to Judah's "covenant with death," and the surrounding religious language indicates that this is neither physical death nor a metaphor for a foreign power but rather a covenant with a deity in place of the one with Yahweh. Isaiah 5:14 describes Sheol, Death's home, as a gaping mouth through which the inhabitants of Jerusalem enter, just as an Ugarit text describes Mot's mouth as stretching from the heavens to the earth; Num 16:30; Ps 141:7; Prov 1:12; and Hab 2:5 also refer to Sheol's "mouth" swallowing people, but Yahweh (ironically) swallows Death (Isa 25:7 [Eng v. 8]). Similarly, the metaphor of Death shepherding people to Sheol (Ps 49:14) echoes an Ugaritic reference to sheep in Mot's mouth.

Connected to the issue of death and the dead, the Ugarit texts may also help clarify an ambiguity with respect to the biblical Rephaim. In some instances, the Rephaim are previous inhabitants of the land, usually characterized as giants, the most famous being King Og of Bashan (Gen 14:5; 15:20; Deut 2:11, 20; 3:11, 13; Josh 12:4; 13:12; 17:15), whereas elsewhere the term refers to the "shades," that is, the dead (Job 26:5; Ps 88:10; Prov 2:18; Isa 14:9; 26:14). Granted, the pre-Israelite residents of Canaan are dead, but that is not what the second group of texts means. However, at Ugarit, the Rephaim constitute two different groups of people. The first are military heroes, a group of elite charioteers, which would be consistent with the giants of old, while elsewhere the Rephaim are the divinized dead kings of Israel, comparable to the biblical shades, especially the rulers in Isa 14:9. Thus, the biblical term has two nuances, just as at Ugarit.

But despite all these parallels between Baʿal and Yahweh, the two were never equated the way El and Yahweh were, and there are important differences between Baʿal at Ugarit and Yahweh in the biblical material. The absence of a battle with the god Death was already noted above. To this we can add that Yahweh does not engage in sexual intercourse, contrary to Baʿal's enthusiastic efforts in that area, nor is Yahweh portrayed as a dying and rising god. Moreover, Baʿal is not a creator deity and, most especially, is not responsible for the origin of humans as Yahweh clearly is.

Two other goddesses from Ugarit remain to be considered. The first is Anat, who is called both Baʿal's wife and his sister, although the latter may be a term of endearment (cf. the repeated address by the male to his bride in the Song of Songs). Despite her sexual involvement with Baʿal on more than one occasion, she is often called "Virgin," although the Ugaritic term may simply denote a woman who has not yet borne children. She plays a major role in the Baʿal myth, burying him after his death at the hands of Mot, then herself killing Mot. She also claims to have slain Leviathan, although the ascription of that deed to Baʿal in another text is more consistent with his battle against Sea (see above). Elsewhere, she desires a bow owned by the human Aqhat, and when he rejects her offer of immortality in exchange, she conspires to have him killed. Both texts are consistent with her common portrayal as a violent, impatient warrior, best represented by a text that describes her wading through a field of battle with blood up to her thighs and the hands and skulls of her enemies attached to her waist.

When it comes to the Bible, there are only a few allusions to her name, with no clear evidence that she was worshiped in Israel. A village called Beth-Anat (House of Anat) is mentioned in Josh 19:38 and Judg 1:33 (see also Beth-Anoth in Josh 15:59), and her name forms part of Anathoth, which refers to both a place (Josh

21:18; Jer 1:1, etc.) and a person (1 Chron 7:8; Neh 10:20). One judge was named Shamgar ben Anat (Judg 3:31; 5:6). This can be compared with two ancient arrowheads from different locations inscribed with the owner's name plus "son of Anat"; the phrase may indicate some type of military guild, although it is impossible to say whether Anat was its patron. These isolated echoes of Anat are surprising in light of her significant role at Ugarit as well as her popularity in the ancient world during the biblical period and beyond, including her worship alongside Yahweh in the Jewish temple at Elephantine (see Chapter 4). As a result, scholars have tried to identify additional references to her and her cult. For instance, in light of the temple dedicated to her that was discovered at Beth-shan, some have linked her to the temple there (1 Sam 31:10) while others have identified her as the winged goddess with a shield (Hos 4:17-19). In Job 31:1 Job vows that he has not looked on a virgin, which is an innocent act in and of itself, and since sexual indiscretions are not mentioned until Job 31:9-12, this may allude to Anat's title of "Virgin" at Ugarit. Others suggest more extensive reflections of Anat in either Deborah (Judges 5) or the woman in the Song of Songs, although the proposed parallels are often quite general or even contrary to the Anat texts from Ugarit. Some find echoes of Anat's blood-soaked journey through a battlefield in texts (e.g., Deut 32:43; Ps 68:24 [Eng v. 23]; Isa 63:3-6) that describe Yahweh wading through blood during battle.

A lesser goddess who often appears alongside Anat is Astarte, spelled Athtart at Ugarit, where she is a hunter (her most common title there is "Athtart of the fields") and a warrior goddess, and is one of Ba'al's consorts (she is also called "Athtart, face of Ba'al"). In the First Testament, her name is spelled as Ashtoreth, a combination of the consonants in her name with the vowels from the Hebrew word *bōšet* (shame). She appears in 1 Kings 11:5, 33 as "the goddess of the Sidonians," one of many foreign deities imported by Solomon, and Josiah defiled the high places that Solomon had set up for her and the others (2 Kings 23:13). Since Astarte was in fact a patron deity of Sidon, Phoenician texts reflect a more immediate source than Ugarit, both geographically and chronologically, for the references to her in the Bible. A plural form of her name (Ashtaroth) is linked to "the Baals" (Judg 2:13; 10:6; 1 Sam 7:4; 12:10) or just "the foreign gods" (1 Sam 7:3); in all these texts the plural simply means "goddesses." The plural also occurs in 1 Sam 31:10, where the Philistines put Saul's "armor in the temple of Ashtaroth" in Beth-shan. The NRSV has the singular "Astarte" (but with a footnote that the Hebrew is actually plural) in order to link the temple to Astarte in particular rather than just "goddesses" in general. However, the actual temple to Anat discovered at Beth-shan (see above) suggests that Anat may be a more likely candidate. As noted in Chapter 1, Astarte, with some influence from Ishtar of Mesopotamia, is probably the Queen of Heaven mentioned in Jer 7:18; 44:17-19, 25.

Before leaving this discussion of Ugarit, we must note that not all attempts to illuminate the biblical texts from the Ugaritic ones have been successful. The most infamous example of this has to do with the prohibition "You shall not boil a kid in its mother's milk" (Exod 23:19; Deut 14:21). One of the early textual discoveries at Ugarit was a tablet that described the chief god El's sexual activities leading to the birth of Dawn and Dusk, with ritual prescriptions on the other side. The excavator filled in letters in a damaged line and translated the result as "cook a kid in milk," which led biblical scholars to explain the biblical law as prohibiting a Canaanite fertility ritual. Unfortunately, the Ugarit text does not mention a *mother's* milk; the word translated as "cook" actually means "slaughter," and the word rendered as "kid" probably means "coriander," like its biblical cognate. In other words, even if the line has been correctly reconstructed, which is debated, it does not mean what the excavator said it did, and the Ugarit text is completely irrelevant for understanding the biblical prohibition. This mistake serves as a reminder of the need not to make hasty comparisons, especially when dealing with a reconstructed text.

# Phoenicia

Phoenicia occupied the territory between the Mediterranean Sea and the Lebanon Mountains, corresponding to modern-day Lebanon. The name, given to the region by the Greeks, comes from the Greek word for "purple," based on the inhabitants' manufacture of purple dye from the Murex snail. The people identified themselves as either Canaanites or by their city of residence.

The geographical restrictions of the area led the Phoenicians onto the water, establishing extensive trade relationships throughout the western Mediterranean. The most famous export was their alphabet, which was adopted by their Semitic neighbors to write their own languages, including Hebrew and the more extensive Aramean, and eventually adapted by the Greeks into what became the precursor to modern Western writing systems.

Although Phoenician cities are mentioned as early as the Egyptian Amarna letters of the Fourteenth Century B.C.E., the region first asserted its independence following the social collapse throughout the Mediterranean ca. 1200 B.C.E., taking advantage of the political vacuum that resulted in part from the migration of the Sea Peoples. The weakening of Egyptian influence in particular was noted in Chapter 2 with respect to the poor treatment given to Wen-Amun. Phoenicia was never a unified country but rather a collection of city-states, the most important being Akka, Aradus, Byblos, Sidon, and Tyre. Often one city took on greater significance and influence in the region; Byblos was dominant in the early years, followed by Sidon in the north and Tyre in the south. Initially, Phoenicia acknowledged Assyrian influence in the area while maintaining a degree of independence. Tiglath-pileser I (ca. 1114–1076 B.C.E.) records an expedition to obtain Lebanese cedar, during which he received tribute from Aradus, Byblos, and Sidon. In the Ninth Century B.C.E., Ashurnasirpal II and Shalmaneser III received tribute from individual Phoenician cities. Beginning with Tiglath-pileser III in the Eighth Century B.C.E., the Assyrians began conquering the region itself, from the north to the south, and incorporating it into the expanding Assyrian Empire. Subsequent revolts by both Sidon and Tyre were easily suppressed, and from that point forward, control of Phoenicia and its cities passed through the succession of Babylonian, Persian, and Greek Empires.

The Bible records a few interactions between the Phoenicians and the Israelites. They are mentioned in a list of various nations that "oppressed" Israel during the period of the Judges (Judg 10:12), but there is no narrative of that oppression. More amiably, King Hiram of Tyre sent carpenters and stone masons to David with cedar to build his palace (2 Sam 5:11). If the inclusion of Tyre and Sidon in David's census (2 Sam 24:6-7) is correct, it may be an indication that Hiram was David's vassal, but there is no other evidence of this, and nothing in 2 Sam 5:11 indicates that Hiram was under any compulsion. This fits with his dealings with Solomon, who paid Hiram for material and artisans for the Temple, followed by a peace treaty between them (1 Kings 5:1-12), although later Hiram rejected the twenty cities Solomon offered as additional payment (1 Kings 9:10-13). Hiram's navy also cooperated with Solomon's in trading expeditions (1 Kings 9:27-28; 10:11, 22). Solomon hosted "Hiram from Tyre" in Jerusalem while the latter constructed pillars and sacred vessels for the temple (1 Kings 7:13-44). His genealogy (his mother is from Naphtali; v. 14) demonstrates that this is not the Tyrian king, and 2 Chron 2:13 eliminates any ambiguity by giving his name as Huram-abi, but the episode indicates that the Temple construction was further indebted to Phoenician craftsmanship.

Religious interactions are presented less positively. The "gods of Sidon" are listed in Judg 10:6 among those the early Israelites worshiped, and Solomon built a temple to "Astarte the goddess of the Sidonians" for one or more of his foreign wives (1 Kings 11:5, 33; 2 Kings 23:13). But the biggest conflict occurred during the reign of Ahab, when his wife, Jezebel, actively promoted the worship of Ba'al in place of Yahweh. She is the daughter of "King Ethbaal of the Sidonians" in 1 Kings 16:31; although there is no recorded king of Sidon with that name, an Ittobaal ruled Tyre at the same time that Ahab and his father, Omri, reigned in Israel. Thus, here "Sidonians" refers to Phoenicians in general rather than inhabitants of that specific city. In keeping with that, Jezebel's Ba'al would have been Melqart, the chief god of Tyre, who was the city's "Lord" (*ba'al*). Elijah led the opposition to Jezebel's efforts, culminating in a competition with Ba'al's prophets on Mount Carmel, at the border between Israel and Tyre, to determine which deity was supreme in Israel, a competition that Yahweh won decisively (see 1 Kings 18 and above).

# Philistia

Philistia is the name given to the Mediterranean coastal plain from the border with Egypt in the south to the Yarkon River in the north. The name comes from the Philistines, who arrived there in the Twelfth Century B.C.E. Their precise origins are uncertain, but their material culture and few examples of writing are Mycenean, indicating roots in the Aegean Sea. They were one of the groups known as the Sea Peoples who migrated from the Aegean after the collapse of the Mycenean civilization, destroying numerous cities and even countries along the way, until ultimately defeated by Ramesses III (ca. 1175 B.C.E.). Egyptian records indicate that he settled three groups, the Sherden, the Tjekker, and the Peleset (i.e., the Philistines), in Ashkelon, Ashdod, and Gaza as his mercenaries. This indicates that the references to Philistines in Genesis and Exodus cannot be historical, since the narrative context in those books predates the Philistines' appearance in the area by centuries.

The Philistines quickly established their independence from Egypt, however, and began to extend their control inland. They added the cities of Ekron and Gath to the other three as a collection of five city-states known as the Philistine Pentapolis. Due to their relatively smaller numbers, they did not replace the local population but rather treated them as their subordinates. Their movement inland inevitably led to conflict with the Israelites, as narrated in the books of Judges and 1 and 2 Samuel. Initial resistance was given by Shamgar ben Anat (Judg 3:31) and Samson (Judges 13–16), but this did not stop the Philistines, who defeated an Israelite army of volunteer militia at Ebenezer, capturing the ark of the covenant and destroying the sanctuary at Shiloh (1 Samuel 4). Despite a subsequent Israelite victory credited to Samuel (1 Sam 7:5-14) that led to a respite from Philistine incursions, the people clamored for a king who could lead an organized military response to the Philistine threat, and Saul was chosen for the task. This attracted Philistine attention again, but despite some successes on the battlefield, Saul was often diverted from dealing with the Philistines by his jealousy over David's greater popularity, forcing David to take refuge with King Achish of Gath (1 Samuel 27). Saul eventually killed himself after losing a battle at Mount Gilboa (1 Samuel 31).

After Saul's death, David was installed as king at Hebron (2 Sam 2:1-4). The Philistines did not oppose him initially, apparently considering him a loyal vassal due to his service to Achish of Gath and an ally in opposing Saul's descendants in the north. But when David was crowned king of all Israel and moved his capital to Jerusalem, the Philistines appeared in force to remove him, only to suffer two defeats at David's hands in the Valley of Rephaim (2 Sam 5:17-25) that broke their power and left Israel the dominant force in the region. The Philistines were not eliminated, however. According to 1 Kings 4:21, they were one of many nations paying tribute to Solomon, suggesting they were a separate territory but subordinate to Israel. Yet isolated skirmishes are recorded in 1 Kings 15:27; 16:15, followed by a more concerted campaign by King Hezekiah (2 Kings 18:8).

The political situation changed dramatically in the latter part of the Eighth Century B.C.E. as the Assyrians expanded westward from Mesopotamia. In 734 B.C.E. Tiglath-pileser III invaded Philistia, with his attention focused on Gaza, which he easily defeated but allowed a degree of independence in return for regular tribute. The other Philistine cities enjoyed the same status, although not without occasional individual revolts, all of which were suppressed by the Assyrians. Sargon II's sieges of Ashdod, Ekron, Gath, and Gaza are all represented in reliefs from his palace at Khorsabad. When the Assyrians fell to the Babylonians, Egypt asserted control over Philistia but was soon driven out by Nebuchadnezzar, who made the region part of his empire. Philistia never regained independence and was controlled in turn by Persia, Greece, and Rome. In any case, by the Sixth Century B.C.E. the Philistines had ceased to be a distinctive ethnic group in the region, but continued to give their name to the coastal plain until Hadrian applied the Latin form *Palestine* to the entire region.

There is no evidence of any Philistine influence on Israelite literature or religion. The first is due to the lack of Philistine texts while the second can be explained by the rapid assimilation of Canaanite culture by the Philistines as a result of their minority status in the region. For instance, female figurines found in the oldest levels of Philistine occupation match similar finds in the Aegean where the Great Goddess was predominant rather than male deities, but within a century, Semitic male deities had taken over. By that point, the primary Philistine deity was Dagon, a member of Semitic pantheons long before the Philistines arrived, and Ba'al-zebub is named as the god of Ekron (2 Kings 1:2); the name is a distortion of Ba'al-zebul (Ba'al is prince). The Philistines also worshiped Semitic goddesses: 1 Sam 31:10 mentions that they had a temple of Astarte (or of goddesses in general) at Beth-shan, and excavations at Ekron have revealed a reference to Asherah, but the female deities were deemed less important than the male ones.

# Aram

Aram was a Semitic nation in southern Syria between the Eleventh and Eighth Centuries B.C.E., with its capital in Damascus. No Aramean documents have been discovered to date, so any information is based on biblical and Assyrian texts. Second Samuel 8:5-6 claims that David took control of Damascus after the Arameans sided with Hadadezer of Zobah (north of Damascus). Subsequently, 1 Kings 11:23-24 states that Rezon, son of one of Hadadezer's servants, installed himself as king in Damascus, and verse 25 indicates that Aram retained its independence throughout the rest of Solomon's rule. The next biblical reference to Aram is set in the early Ninth Century B.C.E., when King Asa of Judah sends treasures to Bar-Hadad I (Ben-Hadad in biblical texts) of Damascus to intervene in his war with King Baasha of Israel, alluding to an otherwise unknown treaty between their parents, with the result that Baasha had to withdraw from the south (1 Kings 15:16-22).

In 1 Kings 20, a certain "Ben-Hadad" besieged Samaria, but was repulsed by Ahab, who subsequently defeated him again at Aphek. Assyrian records indicate that the leader of Aram at this time was named Hadad-idri, and this Ben-Hadad (II) would be identified with him. Then, 1 Kings 22 narrates how three years later "the king of Israel" (Ahab?) and King Jehoshaphat of Judah sought to reclaim Ramoth-Gilead from Aram, only to have Ahab die in the battle. The precise dating of Ahab's reign is disputed, but since he participated in the battle at Qarqar in 853 B.C.E., under any proposed dating these two biblical battles that occurred before and after the one at Qarqar indicate that Israel and Aram put aside their differences long enough to face Shalmaneser III together. However, arguing that an actual Aramean invasion of Israel (1 Kings 20) would not get very far at a time when Ahab could muster two thousand chariots and ten thousand soldiers for the battle at Qarqar, some scholars think these two stories actually deal with later events, namely, the wounding of Ahab's son Joram at Ramoth-Gilead (2 Kings 8:28-29; 9:14-15) and Joash's overthrow of Aramean domination at Aphek (2 Kings 13:17; cf. v. 25).

In any case, Aram led a coalition of twelve kingdoms against Shalmaneser III in 853 B.C.E. (see further in Chapter 1), turning him back at Qarqar. Shalmaneser returned in 849, 848, and 845 B.C.E., but each time was unable to overcome the forces led by Hadad-idri. Then, ca. 842 B.C.E., Hazael seized the throne in Damascus and reopened hostilities with Israel by attacking Ramoth-Gilead, wounding King Joram in the process (2 Kings 8:28-29). This episode is reflected in an Aramaic inscription found at Tel Dan, in which the author says he killed the king of Israel and the king of the "house of David." The actual names of these kings are partially damaged, but are commonly restored as Joram and Ahaziah, respectively (2 Kings 9:21-28 says that Jehu killed them). Of particular interest is the fact that "house of David" does not include an intervening word divider as in most of the inscription, indicating that it was considered a single concept, which many scholars have taken as supporting the historicity of the Davidic dynasty in Judah. Hazael was not able to capitalize on his victory, however, since Shalmaneser returned in 841 B.C.E. Since the earlier coalition had been broken, Hazael was unable to withstand the Assyrian forces alone; they briefly besieged Damascus, although they did not conquer it. Hazael faced the Assyrians again in 838 and 837 B.C.E., after which Shalmaneser focused his attention to his north, allowing Hazael to resume hostilities with his southern neighbors. Exploiting Israelite weakness after Jehu's bloody coup of Joram and purge of his family and their supporters, Hazael seized Israel's territories east of the Jordan River (2 Kings 10:32-33) and soon dominated all of Israel (2 Kings 13:22). He also conquered Gath and marched on Jerusalem; King Jehoash paid him a large tribute, thereby effectively becoming his vassal as well.

Aram's fortunes changed for the worse after Hazael's death and his son Bar-Hadad's (Ben-Hadad [III] in biblical texts) ascension to the throne. King Jehoash of Israel reclaimed the land taken by Hazael (2 Kings 13:25; cf. vv. 4-5), and presumably, Judah regained its independence as well. In addition, the Zakkur Stele notes that Bar-Hadad failed in his invasion of Hamath and Luash, north of Damascus; the stele includes an oracle from "the Lord of the Heavens" announcing his protection and introduced with the words "Do not be afraid," just like many biblical prophecies. Adad-nirari III besieged Damascus circa 794 B.C.E. and received significant amounts of tribute, then Shalmaneser IV attacked Aram (ca. 773 B.C.E.) and also received tribute payments. Meanwhile, 2 Kings 14:25, 28 suggests that Jeroboam II exerted control over Aram during this period as well. Aram's final foray on the international stage occurred under Rezin, who formed a coalition against Assyria that included Israel and Tyre. They invaded Judah in an attempt to force King Ahaz to join them (the Syro-Ephraimite War), but he appealed to Tiglath-pileser III of Assyria, accepting the role of a vassal (2 Kings 16:5-9; cf. Isaiah 7). By 732 B.C.E. Tiglath-pileser had completely conquered Aram, incorporating the area as provinces in his empire. The area subsequently passed under Babylonian control when the latter conquered the Assyrians, and "bands of the Arameans" are mentioned in 2 Kings 24:2 as cooperating with Nebuchadnezzar in the first siege of Jerusalem in 597 B.C.E.

There is little indication of influence from Aram on the content of biblical literature or Israelite religion. Relevant historical inscriptions were noted above, and the Aramaic translation of the Behistun inscription plus the *Proverbs of Ahiqar* from Elephantine were discussed in Chapter 4, while the Aramean pantheon more or less corresponds to that of its Semitic neighbors. However, the Aramaic dialect of Northwest Semitic became the language of international diplomacy, such that it eventually replaced Hebrew as the spoken language in Israel. For instance, 2 Kings 18:26 indicates that during Sennacherib's siege, only the Jerusalem elite could understand Aramaic, whereas Neh 8:8 implies that during the Persian period, the general populace could not understand Hebrew. Some portions of the First Testament are written in Aramaic, namely, Ezra 4:8–6:18; 7:12-26, which claims to quote documents from Cyrus the Great of Persia with respect to the return from exile and rebuilding the Jerusalem temple; Dan 2:4b–7:28; a single sentence in Jer 10:11; and the translation of a place-name in Gen 31:47. Eventually, the Aramaic square script based on the Phoenician alphabet was adopted for written Hebrew as well.

# Ammon

Ammon occupied territory to the east of the Jordan River as far as the Arabian desert and was bounded by the Jabbok River (the Zarqa River today) in the north and the Arnon (Wadi Mujib) in the south, although at times Moab controlled territory to the north of the Arnon. According to Gen 19:38, the inhabitants were descended from Lot and his younger daughter, and for that reason Deut 2:19 orders the Israelites to bypass the region on their way to Canaan. The First Testament narrates a series of interactions between Israel and Ammon. In Judg 3:13 the Ammonites aid Eglon of Moab in conquering the Israelites, while in Judg 10:7 they are named alongside the Philistines, and then alone in verse 9, as oppressors of Israel in punishment for the Israelites worshiping the "gods of the Ammonites" (Judg 10:6); Jephthah's liberation of the Israelites is narrated in Judg 11:1-33. Threats against the people of Jabesh-Gilead by Nahash, king of Ammon, led the newly selected Israelite King Saul to attack the Ammonites (1 Sam 11:1-11), and they are listed as one of his many opponents (1 Sam 14:47). David conquered the capital of Rabbah after King Hanun insulted David's messengers, with David using the inhabitants for forced labor (2 Sam 10:1–11:26; 12:26-31); during the siege, he arranged for Uriah, Bathsheba's husband, to be killed so that David could take her as his own. Later, when David fled Jerusalem during his son Absalom's revolt, Shobi of Rabbah gave him food and shelter (2 Sam 17:27-29), suggesting continued Israelite influence over the area, as does the itinerary of his census takers in 2 Sam 24:5-7. One of Solomon's wives, Naamah, was an Ammonite who gave birth to Solomon's successor, Rehoboam (1 Kings 14:31), and Solomon is said to have worshiped Milcom "the abomination of the Ammonites" (1 Kings 11:5, 33; 2 Kings 23:13; he is called Molech in 1 Kings 11:7).

Ammon participated in the anti-Assyrian coalition that fought Shalmaneser III at Qarqar, indicating that the Ammonites were no longer subject to Israel, but a century later Ammon had become subject to Assyria. King Sanipu is named as paying tribute to Tiglath-pileser III in 733 B.C.E., and a later text records horses delivered by Moab, while Sanipu's son Puduil is named as a vassal to both Sennacherib and Esarhaddon. According to 2 Kings 24:2,

Ammonites fought with the Babylonians when Jehoiakim rebelled in 598 B.C.E., and the Ammonites appear to have taken advantage of Israel's difficulties with Babylon to invade the territory of Gad (Jer 49:1). After the fall of Jerusalem, King Baalis conspired with Ishmael in the murder of Gedaliah, whom the Babylonians had appointed governor, and then sheltered Ishmael afterward (Jer 40:13–41:15). This may be the reason for Ammon's reduction to the status of a Babylonian province in 582 B.C.E., ending any semblance of independence and with it any opportunity to interfere with Judah, which by that point was a Babylonian province. Nonetheless, an Ammonite named Tobiah opposed Nehemiah's rebuilding efforts in the Persian period (Neh 2:10, 19; 3:35 [Eng 4:3]; 4:1 [Eng v. 7]), but as a resident of Jerusalem (Neh 13:4-5), not an outsider. Ammonite women are mentioned as partners in mixed marriages opposed by Ezra and Nehemiah (Ezra 9:1-2; Neh 13:23).

# Moab

Ancient Moab was bordered on the west by the Jordan River and the Dead Sea, on the east by the Arabian desert, on the south by the Zered River (Wadi Hasa), and on the north by the Arnon (Wadi Mujib), although in times of strength its sphere of influence extended farther north. The biblical tradition makes Moab the son of Lot and his older daughter (Gen 19:37) and also narrates a number of interactions between Israel and the land of Moab. As the Israelites approached Canaan, the Amorite King Sihon, who had taken over the area of Heshbon, would not allow them to pass through the area, leading to his defeat by the Israelites (Num 21:21-26). In response King Balak of Moab hired Balaam son of Beor, a seer who saw "the vision of the Almighty" [= Shaddai] in a trance, to curse the Israelites, but God allowed him to utter only blessings on them (Numbers 22–24). Balaam son of Beor also appears in inscriptions of the Eighth Century B.C.E. from Deir Alla in northern Jordan, which present a series of revelations given to Balaam in visions. The content of the oracles is completely different from what is in Numbers, but the Deir Alla texts have two clauses with wording very similar to ones in the biblical texts: the gods come to Balaam at night, just as in Num 22:20, and he then rises the next day (in Num 22:21 he does so "in the morning"). The Deir Alla inscriptions also include references to Shaddayin, the Aramaic plural of Shaddai. Thus, the Deir Alla texts reinforce some aspects of the biblical presentation of Balaam while also suggesting that he had sufficient regional importance to have other traditions about him preserved outside the biblical literature. The biblical story of Balaam is then followed by an episode where the Israelites have sexual relations with Moabite women, who draw them into their worship of Ba'al of Peor (Num 25:1-3; cf. Josh 22:17; Ps 106:28; Hos 9:10), and later traditions blamed Balaam for that.

After the Israelite entry into the land, Judg 3:12-30 records how the Israelites were ruled by Eglon, king of Moab, for eighteen years, presumably as punishment for worshiping Moabite gods (Judg 10:6), until Ehud liberated them. In the book of Ruth, set during the period of the Judges, the Moabite woman Ruth marries Boaz and becomes King David's great-grandmother. This may have provided the basis for David to hide his parents with the king of Moab (1 Sam 22:3-4) when he was fleeing from Saul. Moab is listed as one of the many nations Saul fought (1 Sam 14:47) while David makes Moab his vassal, extracting tribute (2 Sam 8:2). Once again, Solomon is said to have worshiped "Chemosh the abomination of Moab" as part of his accommodation of his foreign wives (1 Kings 11:7, 33; 2 Kings 23:13).

Mesha, king of Moab, paid tribute to Ahab but rebelled when the latter died. The brief notice of this fact in 2 Kings 1:1; 3:4-5 is complemented by Mesha's version inscribed on the Mesha Stele, also known as the Moabite Stone. In it, Mesha states that Omri and "his son" (i.e., Ahab) had been able to occupy Medeba for forty years because Chemosh was "angry with his land," the same explanation given in the Bible for Israel's frequent military defeats. At Chemosh's direction, probably received through a prophet, Mesha drove out the Israelite forces and conquered three towns, slaying the inhabitants in dedication to Ashtar-Chemosh. This is comparable to the biblical "ban" in which the Israelites destroyed defeated populations out of religious fervor and even uses the same Semitic word. Among the items he looted were the "vessels of Yahweh," which is the earliest extrabiblical instance of that divine name; these vessels were also presented ritually to Chemosh. One scholar has even found the phrase "house of

David" in the inscription, as in the Tel Dan inscription described above, but only by filling in one of the consonants in "David" where the text is damaged.

The attempt by Joram (here called Jehoram), Ahab's son, to recapture the lost Moabite territory with the help of Judah and Edom is narrated in 2 Kings 3:6-27. After initial victories by the Israelites, the Moabite king sacrificed his firstborn son in an effort to induce his god to intervene on his behalf; the wording of verse 27 ("great wrath came upon Israel") indicates he succeeded, and the invaders withdrew. After this, 2 Kings 13:20 mentions a Moabite raiding party around the time of the prophet Elisha's death, and 2 Chron 20:1-30 describes how Jerusalem was miraculously saved from an invasion of Moabites and Ammonites during Jehoshaphat's reign; the latter episode is not found in Kings and appears to be legendary.

The subsequent history of Moab can be briefly outlined on the basis of Assyrian records. Tiglath-pileser III records tribute from Moab during his campaigns in the areas in 734–732 B.C.E., and he later received horses from Moab, while Sargon II includes Moab as a conspirator in an unsuccessful revolt led by the Philistine city of Ashdod in 713 B.C.E. Other texts record tribute during the reigns of Sennacherib, Esarhaddon, and Ashurbanipal, and Moab provided troops for Ashurbanipal's wars with Egypt. Second Kings 24:2 includes Moab among those assisting Nebuchadnezzar during his siege of Jerusalem (597 B.C.E.). All of these demonstrate Moab's position as a separate vassal state during this period, but it was incorporated into the Babylonian Empire alongside Ammon in 582 B.C.E. and from there would have been under the control of Persia and Greece. There are passing references to mixed marriages with Moabite women during the time of Ezra and Nehemiah (Ezra 9:1-2; Neh 13:23) but no existing historical references to Moab as such during this period. The region was eventually overrun by Arab tribes.

# Edom

The territory of Edom ran from the Zered River (Wadi Hasa) at the southern end of the Dead Sea through the Arabah Valley to the Gulf of Aqaba. In Gen 14:6; 36:20; and Deut 2:12, 22 the region's early inhabitants are called "Horites," who were later displaced by the Edomites. The mistaken identification of the Horites with the Hurrians of Mitanni was discussed earlier. *Horite* probably derives from *hurru*, an Egyptian name for Canaan, influenced by the similarity to the Hebrew word *hôr* ("cave") and the belief that Edomites lived in caves (Obadiah 3). In the biblical tradition the Edomites were considered the descendants of Esau, Isaac's brother.

As with Ammon and Moab, most of our knowledge of Edom is based on biblical texts, with some additional information from Egypt, Assyria, and Babylon; no historical records from Edom itself have been discovered to date. Scattered Egyptian texts from the Fifteenth to the Twelfth Centuries B.C.E. mention Edom and Seir; the latter was originally designated the southern portion of Edom but eventually became a synonym for the entire land. Some of these texts refer to *Shasu* in these areas. The term is often translated as "wanderers" or "nomads," but the description of their activities indicates that it more likely means "plunderers," designating a social group comparable to the *'apiru* discussed in Chapter 2. The list of Edomite kings ruling in succession found in Gen 36:31-39 is a later Israelite reconstruction that is not based on any historical record, dealing with a period when Edom did not have kings. Thus, in Num 20:14-21 an unnamed Edomite king denies the Israelites passage on the journey from Egypt to Canaan, forcing them to go around the territory.

Edom and its inhabitants play no role in the period of the Judges but are mentioned in passing as one of Saul's war opponents (1 Sam 14:47). David's campaign in 2 Sam 8:13-14 (see also 1 Kings 11:15-16) is presented as part of his subjugation of the Transjordanian states, including Ammon and Moab, with the result that the Edomites became his vassals. Solomon took an Edomite wife (1 Kings 11:1), but their gods are not included in the usual lists of those for whom he built sanctuaries; he is also said to have established a navy in Edomite territory (1 Kings 9:26). The implied domination of Edom by Israel continued at least until the time of Jehoshaphat, who exercised control through a deputy rather than an Edomite king (1 Kings 22:47). Jehoram of Israel's failed attempt to reclaim Moab after Mesha's revolt included an unnamed king of Edom (2 Kings 3:9, 12, 26), but this is contradicted by the claim that Edom successfully established a monarchy and drove out the

Israelites under Joram of Judah (2 Kings 8:20-22). The inclusion of an Edomite king in the first episode may be the result of the route taken by Jehoram and his southern ally, Jehoshaphat, but in any case the assertion in 2 Kings 8:22 that "Edom has been in revolt . . . to this day" implies continued independence until the time of the passage's composition. Second Kings 14:7 records a raid by Amaziah of Judah but no continued presence. However, around the same time Edom paid tribute to the Assyrian King Adad-nirari III, indicating that Edom's position was weakened, a fact reinforced by Uzziah of Jerusalem's reestablishing an Israelite presence at Elath on the Gulf of Aqaba (2 Kings 14:22). This area was reclaimed by the Edomites during the Syro-Ephraimite War, ca. 734 B.C.E. (2 Kings 16:6), and 2 Chron 28:17 indicates that Edom also attacked Judah.

After the anti-Assyrian revolt led by Rezin of Aram and Pekah of Judah was defeated, Edom is listed by Tiglath-pileser III as one of the many regional powers that paid him tribute. Edom's status as an Assyrian vassal is confirmed by additional tribute paid to Sargon II, Sennacherib, and Esarhaddon and the presence of Edomite conscripts in Ashurbanipal's army. Edom appears to have retained this status under Babylon once Nebuchadnezzar established his control over the area in 605 B.C.E., but 2 Kings 24:2 does not include the Edomites with the Arameans, Ammonites, and Moabites as participating in Nebuchadnezzar's first siege of Jerusalem. Edomite envoys are listed at a meeting with Zedekiah in 594 B.C.E. to discuss a rebellion (Jer 27:3), but when the time came, according to Ps 137:7 and Obadiah 11-14, Edom joined Babylon in the sack of Jerusalem. Other more general condemnations of Edom (e.g., Isaiah 34; Ezek 25:12; 35:3, 15; Lam 4:21-22; Joel 4:19 [Eng 3:19]; Mal 1:2-5) are generally read in light of the first two texts, and the extrabiblical 1 Esd 4:45 goes so far as to attribute the city's burning to Edom rather than Babylon. If Edomite cooperation with Babylon is historical, that may explain why it retained independence as a vassal kingdom after 582 B.C.E., when Ammon and Moab were incorporated directly into the Babylonian Empire. However, this changed circa 552 B.C.E. with an incursion into Edom recorded by Nabonidus in his chronicle.

Little is known about the territory during the Persian and Hellenistic periods. Some suggest that Geshem the Arab was ruling

Edom during Nehemiah's time, but the four verses that mention him (Neh 2:19; 6:1, 2, 6) do not actually say that and give no indication of his location. The only thing that can be said with certainty is that by the beginning of the Hellenistic period, the Nabateans had taken over the area.

# Midian

The land of Midian lay southeast of Edom along the eastern shore of the Gulf of Aqaba, with the two nations' southern and northern boundaries overlapping at times. It was here that Moses had his initial encounter with Yahweh. Later biblical traditions associated the Midianites with sites farther north in the Transjordan region: Gen 36:35 situates them in Moab, in Num 22:5, 7 Midianite and Moabite elders go to bring Balaam to Moab in order to curse the Israelites, and Midianite women are mentioned during the incident of Ba'al of Peor at Shittim (Num 25:6, 14-15, 18). Moses subsequently ordered the Midianites' extermination in Numbers 31 (cf. Josh 13:21), but they remained to oppress the Israelites during the time of Gideon (Judges 6–8).

The Midianites are most important for Israelite religion with respect to Moses' interactions with them in the south. A number of scholars have argued on the basis of these texts that Yahweh was originally a Midianite deity. Moses first encounters Yahweh while tending the flocks of his father-in-law, Jethro, "the priest of Midian," and the mountain is not only called Horeb, rather than Mount Sinai, but is also designated "the mountain of God" before he has that encounter (Exod 3:1); this has been taken to mean that it was already a holy site, although the phrase could simply convey the narrator's assessment of its sanctity after the fact. More telling is that after the Israelites escaped from Egypt, the celebratory sacrificial meal at the mountain was presided over by Jethro (Exod 18:12) rather than Aaron, the high priest of Israel. In addition, we can note that the "War Theophanies" place Yahweh far south of Israel when he is asked to come and fight on behalf of Israel, despite the tradition that Yahweh dwelt in the Jerusalem temple. For instance, in Ps 68:18 (Eng. v. 17) he starts out from Sinai, while Deut 33:2-3 mentions Sinai, Seir (southern Edom but earlier considered Midianite territory), and Mount Paran (in the Sinai) in parallel; related to this last are Judg 5:4-5, with Seir, Edom, and Sinai, and Hab 3:3, with Teman and Paran. This last text also calls to mind the mention of "Yahweh of Teman" in an inscription dated Eighth Century B.C.E. from Kuntillet Ajrûd, whose invocation alongside "Yahweh of Samaria" shows the survival of Yahweh's southern associations well after the settlement farther north.

There is also some archaeological support for a link between Yahweh and Midian. Egyptian texts from the middle of the Second Millennium B.C.E. mention "the land of the Shasu of Yahu." This occurs in sequence with five other place-names, including Seir, also named in the War Theophanies above, and Reuel, which echoes one version of the name of Moses' father-in-law (Exod 2:18). In keeping with the sequence, Yahu in this text indicates a geographical location rather than a deity, but it is possible that a group could name its territory after its god or the reverse, although that cannot be proved. Nevertheless, the similarity to the divine name revealed to Moses in the same geographical region is suggestive. To this we can add points of contact between aspects of Midianite and Israelite religion, as reflected in the Midianite takeover (ca. 1150 B.C.E.) of an Egyptian copper mine at Timna, about thirty kilometers north of the Gulf of Aqaba. In an accompanying shrine, the existing images of Hathor were defaced, suggesting an opposition to images similar to that in the Ten Commandments. At the same time a tent shrine and a copper snake were installed, which recall the "tent of meeting" and the snake Moses erected in the wilderness, which was later preserved in the Jerusalem temple as "Nehushtan" (see Num 21:6-9; 2 Kings 18:4). This does not prove Midianite influence on the Israelites, since the reverse process and independent traditions are both plausible alternate interpretations, but when combined with the other points it does support the view that Yahweh was first encountered as a Midianite deity far from the land of Israel. If correct, that has additional implications for the original distinction between El and Yahweh discussed above under "Ugarit," especially since Yahweh is not named in any existing West-Semitic pantheon, and there is no indication that El was ever considered active outside the land of Canaan.

125

# Index of Ancient Texts

## Biblical Texts

## Genesis

| | |
|---|---|
| 1 | 8, 35 |
| 1:2 | 8, 107 |
| 1:6-10 | 107 |
| 1:14 | 8 |
| 1:26 | 9 |
| 3:24 | 15 |
| 4:7 | 15 |
| 5:27 | 4 |
| 6–9 | 9 |
| 6:3 | 4 |
| 6:14 | 10 |
| 8:20 | 4 |
| 8:21 | 10 |
| 10:15 | 53 |
| 11 | 4, 27 |
| 11:4 | 27 |
| 12:10-20 | 92 |
| 14:5 | 107 |
| 14:6 | 90, 121 |
| 14:18-22 | 99 |
| 14:19 | 60, 99 |
| 15:2-3 | 90 |
| 15:9-18 | 89 |
| 15:20 | 107 |
| 16 | 90 |
| 16:13 | 99, 100 |
| 19:37 | 119 |
| 19:38 | 118 |
| 20:1-18 | 92 |
| 20:12 | 92 |
| 21:1-21 | 90 |
| 21:33 | 99 |
| 23 | 53 |
| 23:10 | 53 |
| 24 | 90 |
| 24:58 | 90 |
| 25:9 | 53 |
| 26:1-11 | 92 |
| 26:34 | 53 |
| 27 | 91 |
| 27:46 | 53 |
| 29 | 90 |
| 31 | 91, 94 |
| 31:19 | 91 |
| 31:30 | 91 |
| 31:32 | 91 |
| 31:47 | 117 |
| 32:23-32 | 56 |

33:20 . . . . . . . . . . . . . . . . . . . . . . 100
35:7 . . . . . . . . . . . . . . . . . . . . 99, 100
36:2 . . . . . . . . . . . . . . . . . . . . . . . 53
36:20 . . . . . . . . . . . . . . . . . . . 90, 121
36:20-30 . . . . . . . . . . . . . . . . . . . . 90
36:31-39 . . . . . . . . . . . . . . . . . . . 122
36:35 . . . . . . . . . . . . . . . . . . . . . 124
38 . . . . . . . . . . . . . . . . . . . . . . 11, 90
38:15 . . . . . . . . . . . . . . . . . . . . . . 98
38:21-22 . . . . . . . . . . . . . . . . . . . . 98
38:24 . . . . . . . . . . . . . . . . . . . . . . 98
39:7-20 . . . . . . . . . . . . . . . . . . . . . 48
44:5 . . . . . . . . . . . . . . . . . . . . . . . . 5
46:3 . . . . . . . . . . . . . . . . . . . . . . 100
48–49 . . . . . . . . . . . . . . . . . . . . . . 91
49:24 . . . . . . . . . . . . . . . . . . . . . 101
49:25 . . . . . . . . . . . . . . . . . . . . . 101
49:26 . . . . . . . . . . . . . . . . . . . . . 101

## Exodus

1:11 . . . . . . . . . . . . . . . . . . . . . . . 37
2:18 . . . . . . . . . . . . . . . . . . . . . . 125
3:1 . . . . . . . . . . . . . . . . . . . . . . . 124
3:6 . . . . . . . . . . . . . . . . . . . . . . . 101
3:8 . . . . . . . . . . . . . . . . . . . . . . . 54
3:17 . . . . . . . . . . . . . . . . . . . . . . . 54
6:3 . . . . . . . . . . . . . . . . . . . . . . . 101
13:5 . . . . . . . . . . . . . . . . . . . . . . . 54
13:12 . . . . . . . . . . . . . . . . . . . . . . 89
18:12 . . . . . . . . . . . . . . . . . . . . . 124
20:2a . . . . . . . . . . . . . . . . . . . . . . 58
20:2b . . . . . . . . . . . . . . . . . . . . . . 58
20:4 . . . . . . . . . . . . . . . . . . . . . . 103
20:23-26 . . . . . . . . . . . . . . . . . . . . 11
20:23–23:19 . . . . . . . . . . . . . . . . . . 11
21:2–22:16 . . . . . . . . . . . . . . . . . . . 11
21:18-19 . . . . . . . . . . . . . . . . . . . . 55
21:28-32 . . . . . . . . . . . . . . . . . 11–12
21:35 . . . . . . . . . . . . . . . . . . . . . . 10
22:17–23:19 . . . . . . . . . . . . . . . . . . 11
22:20-23 . . . . . . . . . . . . . . . . . . . . 11

23:19 . . . . . . . . . . . . . . . . . . . . . 110
24:3-4 . . . . . . . . . . . . . . . . . . . . . 58
24:7-8 . . . . . . . . . . . . . . . . . . . . . 58
25:18-20 . . . . . . . . . . . . . . . . . . . . 15
28:30 . . . . . . . . . . . . . . . . . . . . . . . 6

## Leviticus

1:4 . . . . . . . . . . . . . . . . . . . . . . . 55
3:2 . . . . . . . . . . . . . . . . . . . . . . . 55
3:8 . . . . . . . . . . . . . . . . . . . . . . . 55
3:13 . . . . . . . . . . . . . . . . . . . . . . . 55
8:8 . . . . . . . . . . . . . . . . . . . . . . . . 6
14:2-7 . . . . . . . . . . . . . . . . . . . . . 55
14:48-53 . . . . . . . . . . . . . . . . . . . . 55
16 . . . . . . . . . . . . . . . . . . . . . . . . 55
16:8 . . . . . . . . . . . . . . . . . . . . . . . . 5
16:8-10 . . . . . . . . . . . . . . . . . . . . . 15
16:14-33 . . . . . . . . . . . . . . . . . . . . 60
16:21-22 . . . . . . . . . . . . . . . . . . . . 15
18:9 . . . . . . . . . . . . . . . . . . . . . . . 92
18:11 . . . . . . . . . . . . . . . . . . . . . . 92
20:17 . . . . . . . . . . . . . . . . . . . . . . 92
20:27 . . . . . . . . . . . . . . . . . . . . . . 57
25:8-17 . . . . . . . . . . . . . . . . . . . . . . 6
25:10 . . . . . . . . . . . . . . . . . . . . . . . 6
26 . . . . . . . . . . . . . . . . . . . . . . . . 58
26:1-13 . . . . . . . . . . . . . . . . . . . . . 58
26:14-33 . . . . . . . . . . . . . . . . . . 58, 60

## Numbers

3:6-10 . . . . . . . . . . . . . . . . . . . . . 55
3:32 . . . . . . . . . . . . . . . . . . . . . . . 55
3:38 . . . . . . . . . . . . . . . . . . . . . . . 55
16:9 . . . . . . . . . . . . . . . . . . . . . . . 55
16:30 . . . . . . . . . . . . . . . . . . . . . 107
18:2-4 . . . . . . . . . . . . . . . . . . . . . 55
18:26-28 . . . . . . . . . . . . . . . . . . . . 55
20:14-21 . . . . . . . . . . . . . . . . . . . 122
21:6-9 . . . . . . . . . . . . . . . . . . . . . 125
21:21-26 . . . . . . . . . . . . . . . . . . . 119

22–24 . . . . . . . . . . . . . . . . . . . . . . 119
22:5 . . . . . . . . . . . . . . . . . . . . . . . 124
22:7 . . . . . . . . . . . . . . . . . . . . . . . 124
22:20 . . . . . . . . . . . . . . . . . . . . . . 119
22:21 . . . . . . . . . . . . . . . . . . . . . . 120
24:3-4 . . . . . . . . . . . . . . . . . . . . . . 39
24:4 . . . . . . . . . . . . . . . . . . . . . . . 87
24:15-16 . . . . . . . . . . . . . . . . . . . . 39
24:16 . . . . . . . . . . . . . . . . . . 87, 100
25:1-3 . . . . . . . . . . . . . . . . . . . . . 120
25:6 . . . . . . . . . . . . . . . . . . . . . . . 124
25:14-15 . . . . . . . . . . . . . . . . . . . 124
25:18 . . . . . . . . . . . . . . . . . . . . . . 124
27:21 . . . . . . . . . . . . . . . . . . . . . . . 6
31 . . . . . . . . . . . . . . . . . . . . . . . . 124
34:7-9 . . . . . . . . . . . . . . . . . . . . . . 54

# Deuteronomy

1–4 . . . . . . . . . . . . . . . . . . . . . . . . 58
2:11 . . . . . . . . . . . . . . . . . . . . . . . 107
2:12 . . . . . . . . . . . . . . . . . . . 90, 121
2:19 . . . . . . . . . . . . . . . . . . . . . . . 118
2:20 . . . . . . . . . . . . . . . . . . . . . . . 107
2:22 . . . . . . . . . . . . . . . . . . . 90, 121
3:11 . . . . . . . . . . . . . . . . . . . . . . . 107
3:13 . . . . . . . . . . . . . . . . . . . . . . . 107
4:26 . . . . . . . . . . . . . . . . . . . . . . . 59
5–26 . . . . . . . . . . . . . . . . . . . . . . . 58
7:1 . . . . . . . . . . . . . . . . . . . . . . . . 54
7:13 . . . . . . . . . . . . . . . . . . . . . . . 89
10:1-5 . . . . . . . . . . . . . . . . . . . . . . 58
14:21 . . . . . . . . . . . . . . . . . . . . . . 110
16:21 . . . . . . . . . . . . . . . . . . . . . . 102
21:1-2 . . . . . . . . . . . . . . . . . . . . . . 55
22:23-27 . . . . . . . . . . . . . . . . . . . . 55
23:18-19 [Eng vv. 17-18] . . . . . . . 98
24:1-2 . . . . . . . . . . . . . . . . . . . . . . 55
25:5 . . . . . . . . . . . . . . . . . . . . 91, 94
25:5-6 . . . . . . . . . . . . . . . . . . . . . . 55
25:5-10 . . . . . . . . . . . . . . . . . . 11, 90
27–28 . . . . . . . . . . . . . . . . . . . 59, 60

27:2-3 . . . . . . . . . . . . . . . . . . . . . . 58
27:22 . . . . . . . . . . . . . . . . . . . . . . . 92
28:4 . . . . . . . . . . . . . . . . . . . . . . . 89
28:18 . . . . . . . . . . . . . . . . . . . . . . . 89
28:23-24 . . . . . . . . . . . . . . . . . . . . 60
28:27 . . . . . . . . . . . . . . . . . . . . . . . 60
28:28 . . . . . . . . . . . . . . . . . . . . . . . 60
28:32 . . . . . . . . . . . . . . . . . . . . . . . 60
28:38 . . . . . . . . . . . . . . . . . . . . . . . 60
28:51 . . . . . . . . . . . . . . . . . . . . . . . 89
28:52-53 . . . . . . . . . . . . . . . . . . . . 60
28:53 . . . . . . . . . . . . . . . . . . . . . . . 60
31:9-13 . . . . . . . . . . . . . . . . . . . . . 58
31:10-13 . . . . . . . . . . . . . . . . . . . . 59
31:19-22 . . . . . . . . . . . . . . . . . . . . 59
31:24-26 . . . . . . . . . . . . . . . . . 58, 59
31:26-28 . . . . . . . . . . . . . . . . . . . . 59
32:39-43 . . . . . . . . . . . . . . . . . . . . 59
32:43 . . . . . . . . . . . . . . . . . . . . . . 109
33 . . . . . . . . . . . . . . . . . . . . . . . . . 91
33:2-3 . . . . . . . . . . . . . . . . . . . . . 124
33:8 . . . . . . . . . . . . . . . . . . . . . . . . 6
33:26 . . . . . . . . . . . . . . . . . . . . . . 105

# Joshua

1:4 . . . . . . . . . . . . . . . . . . . . . . . . 54
1:8 . . . . . . . . . . . . . . . . . . . . . . . . 59
7 . . . . . . . . . . . . . . . . . . . . . . . . . . 5
12:4 . . . . . . . . . . . . . . . . . . . . . . . 107
13:5 . . . . . . . . . . . . . . . . . . . . . . . 54
13:12 . . . . . . . . . . . . . . . . . . . . . . 107
13:21 . . . . . . . . . . . . . . . . . . . . . . 124
15:59 . . . . . . . . . . . . . . . . . . . . . . 108
17:15 . . . . . . . . . . . . . . . . . . . . . . 107
18:6 . . . . . . . . . . . . . . . . . . . . . . . . 5
19:38 . . . . . . . . . . . . . . . . . . . . . . 108
21:18 . . . . . . . . . . . . . . . . . . . . . . 109
22:17 . . . . . . . . . . . . . . . . . . . . . . 120
24 . . . . . . . . . . . . . . . . . . . . . . . . . 59
24:2a . . . . . . . . . . . . . . . . . . . . . . . 59
24:2b-13 . . . . . . . . . . . . . . . . . . . . 59

24:14 . . . . . . . . . . . . . . . . . . . . . . . 59
24:17-18 . . . . . . . . . . . . . . . . . . 59
24:19-20 . . . . . . . . . . . . . . . . . . 59
24:22 . . . . . . . . . . . . . . . . . . . . . . . 59
24:23 . . . . . . . . . . . . . . . . . . . . . . . 59
24:25 . . . . . . . . . . . . . . . . . . . . . . . 59
24:25-26a . . . . . . . . . . . . . . . . . 59
24:26b . . . . . . . . . . . . . . . . . . . . 59
24:26b-27 . . . . . . . . . . . . . . . . . 59

## Judges

. . . . . . . . . . . . . . . . . . . . . . . 5, 113
1:33 . . . . . . . . . . . . . . . . . . . . . . . 108
2:13 . . . . . . . . . . . . . . . . . . . . . . . 109
3:7 . . . . . . . . . . . . . . . . . . . . . . . 102
3:12-30 . . . . . . . . . . . . . . . . . . . 120
3:13 . . . . . . . . . . . . . . . . . . . . . . . 118
3:31 . . . . . . . . . . . . . . . . . . 109, 113
5 . . . . . . . . . . . . . . . . . . . . . . . . 109
5:4-5 . . . . . . . . . . . . . . . . . . . . . . . 125
5:6 . . . . . . . . . . . . . . . . . . . . . . . 109
5:17b . . . . . . . . . . . . . . . . . . . . . 96
6–8 . . . . . . . . . . . . . . . . . . . . . . . 124
8:33 . . . . . . . . . . . . . . . . . . . . . . . 100
9:4 . . . . . . . . . . . . . . . . . . . . . . . 100
9:46 . . . . . . . . . . . . . . . . . . . 99, 100
10:1 . . . . . . . . . . . . . . . . . . . . . . . 57
10:3-4 . . . . . . . . . . . . . . . . . . . . . 57
10:6 . . . . . . . . . 109, 112, 118, 120
10:7 . . . . . . . . . . . . . . . . . . . . . . . 118
10:9 . . . . . . . . . . . . . . . . . . . . . . . 118
10:12 . . . . . . . . . . . . . . . . . . . . . . 111
11:1-33 . . . . . . . . . . . . . . . . . . . 118
12:8-9 . . . . . . . . . . . . . . . . . . . . . 57
12:11 . . . . . . . . . . . . . . . . . . . . . . 57
12:13-14 . . . . . . . . . . . . . . . . . . 57
13–16 . . . . . . . . . . . . . . . . . . . . . 113

## Ruth

4 . . . . . . . . . . . . . . . . . . . . . . . 11, 90

## 1 Samuel

. . . . . . . . . . . . . . . . . . . . . . . 5, 113
4 . . . . . . . . . . . . . . . . . . . . . . . 113
5–6 . . . . . . . . . . . . . . . . . . . . . . . 56
7:3 . . . . . . . . . . . . . . . . . . . . . . . 109
7:4 . . . . . . . . . . . . . . . . . . . . . . . 109
7:5-14 . . . . . . . . . . . . . . . . . . . . . 113
9:5-10 . . . . . . . . . . . . . . . . . . . . . 88
9:17 . . . . . . . . . . . . . . . . . . . . . . . 88
10:5 . . . . . . . . . . . . . . . . . . . . . . . 87
10:5-13 . . . . . . . . . . . . . . . . . 39, 87
10:10 . . . . . . . . . . . . . . . . . . . . . . 87
10:20-21 . . . . . . . . . . . . . . . . . . . 5
11:1-11 . . . . . . . . . . . . . . . . . . . 118
12:10 . . . . . . . . . . . . . . . . . . . . . . 109
14:9-10 . . . . . . . . . . . . . . . . . . . . 5
14:24-42 . . . . . . . . . . . . . . . . . . 6
14:41 . . . . . . . . . . . . . . . . . . . . . . 6
14:47 . . . . . . . . . . . . . 118, 120, 122
19:18-24 . . . . . . . . . . . . . . . . 39, 87
22:3-4 . . . . . . . . . . . . . . . . . . . . 120
27 . . . . . . . . . . . . . . . . . . . . . . . 113
28 . . . . . . . . . . . . . . . . . . . . . . . 57
28:6 . . . . . . . . . . . . . . . . . . . . . . . 6
31 . . . . . . . . . . . . . . . . . . . . . . . 113
31:10 . . . . . . . . . . . . . 109, 110, 115

## 2 Samuel

. . . . . . . . . . . . . . . . . . . . . . . 5, 113
2:1-4 . . . . . . . . . . . . . . . . . . . . . . 113
5:11 . . . . . . . . . . . . . . . . . . . 111, 112
5:17-25 . . . . . . . . . . . . . . . . . . . 114
5:19 . . . . . . . . . . . . . . . . . . . . . . . 88
5:19-20 . . . . . . . . . . . . . . . . . . . . 20
5:23 . . . . . . . . . . . . . . . . . . . . . . . 88
7 . . . . . . . . . . . . . . . . . . . . . . . . 25
8:2 . . . . . . . . . . . . . . . . . . . . . . . 120
8:5-6 . . . . . . . . . . . . . . . . . . . . . . 115
8:9-10 . . . . . . . . . . . . . . . . . . . . . 54
8:13-14 . . . . . . . . . . . . . . . . . . . 122

10:1–11:26 . . . . . . . . . . . . . . . . . . 118
12:26-31 . . . . . . . . . . . . . . . . . . . 118
17:27-29 . . . . . . . . . . . . . . . . . . . 118
24:5-7 . . . . . . . . . . . . . . . . . . . . . 118
24:6 . . . . . . . . . . . . . . . . . . . . . . . . 54
24:6-7 . . . . . . . . . . . . . . . . . . . . . 111

# 1 Kings

. . . . . . . . . . . . . . . . . . . . . . . . . . . 5
4:21 . . . . . . . . . . . . . . . . . . . . . . . 114
5:1-12 . . . . . . . . . . . . . . . . . . . . . 112
6:23-28 . . . . . . . . . . . . . . . . . . . . . 15
7:13-44 . . . . . . . . . . . . . . . . . . . . 112
7:14 . . . . . . . . . . . . . . . . . . . . . . . 112
9:10-13 . . . . . . . . . . . . . . . . . . . . 112
9:26 . . . . . . . . . . . . . . . . . . . . . . . 122
9:27-28 . . . . . . . . . . . . . . . . . . . . 112
10:11 . . . . . . . . . . . . . . . . . . . . . . 112
10:22 . . . . . . . . . . . . . . . . . . . . . . 112
10:29 . . . . . . . . . . . . . . . . . . . . . . . 54
11:1 . . . . . . . . . . . . . . . . . . . 54, 122
11:5 . . . . . . . . . . . . . . 109, 112, 118
11:7 . . . . . . . . . . . . . . . . . . 118, 120
11:15-16 . . . . . . . . . . . . . . . . . . . 122
11:23-24 . . . . . . . . . . . . . . . . . . . 115
11:25 . . . . . . . . . . . . . . . . . . . . . . 115
11:33 . . . . . . . . . . 109, 112, 118, 120
11:40 . . . . . . . . . . . . . . . . . . . . . . . 40
14:24 . . . . . . . . . . . . . . . . . . . . . . . 98
14:25 . . . . . . . . . . . . . . . . . . . . . . . 40
14:26 . . . . . . . . . . . . . . . . . . . . . . . 40
14:31 . . . . . . . . . . . . . . . . . . . . . . 118
15:12 . . . . . . . . . . . . . . . . . . . . . . . 98
15:13 . . . . . . . . . . . . . . . . . . . . . . 102
15:16-22 . . . . . . . . . . . . . . . . . . . 115
15:27 . . . . . . . . . . . . . . . . . . . . . . 114
16:15 . . . . . . . . . . . . . . . . . . . . . . 114
16:31 . . . . . . . . . . . . . . . . . . . . . . 112
18 . . . . . . . . . . . . . . . . . . . 104, 112
18:1 . . . . . . . . . . . . . . . . . . . . . . . 104
18:19 . . . . . . . . . . . . . . . . . 102, 103

18:21 . . . . . . . . . . . . . . . . . . . . . . . 39
18:24 . . . . . . . . . . . . . . . . . . . 93, 104
18:28-29 . . . . . . . . . . . . . . . . . . . . 87
18:38 . . . . . . . . . . . . . . . . . . . . . . 104
20 . . . . . . . . . . . . . . . . . . . . . . . . 115
20:32-33 . . . . . . . . . . . . . . . . . . . . . 5
20:35 . . . . . . . . . . . . . . . . . . . . . . . 87
22 . . . . . . . . . . . . . . . . . . . . . . . . 115
22:6 . . . . . . . . . . . . . . . . . . . . . . . . 20
22:6-15 . . . . . . . . . . . . . . . . . . . . . 88
22:47 [Eng v. 46] . . . . . . . . 98, 122

# 2 Kings

. . . . . . . . . . . . . . . . . . . . . . . . . . . 5
1:1 . . . . . . . . . . . . . . . . . . . . . . . 120
1:2 . . . . . . . . . . . . . . . . . . . . . . . 114
2:3 . . . . . . . . . . . . . . . . . . . . . . . . 87
2:5 . . . . . . . . . . . . . . . . . . . . . . . . 87
2:7 . . . . . . . . . . . . . . . . . . . . . . . . 87
2:15 . . . . . . . . . . . . . . . . . . . . . . . 87
3:4 . . . . . . . . . . . . . . . . . . . . . . . . 96
3:4-5 . . . . . . . . . . . . . . . . . . . . . . 120
3:6-27 . . . . . . . . . . . . . . . . . . . . . 121
3:9 . . . . . . . . . . . . . . . . . . . . . . . 122
3:12 . . . . . . . . . . . . . . . . . . . . . . . 122
3:15 . . . . . . . . . . . . . . . . . . . . 39, 87
3:26 . . . . . . . . . . . . . . . . . . . . . . . 122
3:27 . . . . . . . . . . . . . . . . . . . . . . . 121
4:1 . . . . . . . . . . . . . . . . . . . . . . . . 87
4:38 . . . . . . . . . . . . . . . . . . . . . . . 87
5:11 . . . . . . . . . . . . . . . . . . . . . . . 93
5:22 . . . . . . . . . . . . . . . . . . . . . . . 87
7:6 . . . . . . . . . . . . . . . . . . . . . . . . 54
8:20-22 . . . . . . . . . . . . . . . . . . . . 123
8:22 . . . . . . . . . . . . . . . . . . . . . . . 123
8:28-29 . . . . . . . . . . . . . . . . . . . . 116
9:1 . . . . . . . . . . . . . . . . . . . . . . . . 87
9:11 . . . . . . . . . . . . . . . . . . . . . . . 88
9:14-15 . . . . . . . . . . . . . . . . . . . . 116
9:21-28 . . . . . . . . . . . . . . . . . . . . 116
10:24 . . . . . . . . . . . . . . . . . . . . . . . 55

10:30 . . . . . . . . . . . . . . . . . . . . . . . 103
10:32-33 . . . . . . . . . . . . . . . . . . . . 116
13:4-5 . . . . . . . . . . . . . . . . . . . . . . 116
13:6 . . . . . . . . . . . . . . . . . . . . . . . . 103
13:17 . . . . . . . . . . . . . . . . . . . . . . . 116
13:20 . . . . . . . . . . . . . . . . . . . . . . . 121
13:22 . . . . . . . . . . . . . . . . . . . . . . . 116
13:25 . . . . . . . . . . . . . . . . . . . . . . . 116
14:7 . . . . . . . . . . . . . . . . . . . . . . . . 123
14:22 . . . . . . . . . . . . . . . . . . . . . . . 123
14:25 . . . . . . . . . . . . . . . . . . . . . . . 117
14:28 . . . . . . . . . . . . . . . . . . . . . . . 117
15:19-21 . . . . . . . . . . . . . . . . . . . . . 17
16:5-9 . . . . . . . . . . . . . . . . . . . 17, 117
16:6 . . . . . . . . . . . . . . . . . . . . . . . . 123
17:4 . . . . . . . . . . . . . . . . . . . . . . . . . 40
17:10 . . . . . . . . . . . . . . . . . . . . . . . 102
17:24 . . . . . . . . . . . . . . . . . . . . . . . . 17
18 . . . . . . . . . . . . . . . . . . . . . . . . . . 19
18:4 . . . . . . . . . . . . . . . . . . . . . . . . 125
18:7-8 . . . . . . . . . . . . . . . . . . . . . . . 18
18:8 . . . . . . . . . . . . . . . . . . . . . . . . 114
18:13-14 . . . . . . . . . . . . . . . . . . . . . 18
18:14-16 . . . . . . . . . . . . . . . . . . . . . 19
18:26 . . . . . . . . . . . . . . . . . . . . . . . 117
19:2-7 . . . . . . . . . . . . . . . . . . . . . . . 88
19:9 . . . . . . . . . . . . . . . . . . . . . . . . . 19
19:35-36 . . . . . . . . . . . . . . . . . . . . . 19
19:37 . . . . . . . . . . . . . . . . . . . . . . . . 20
20:12 . . . . . . . . . . . . . . . . . . . . . . . . 18
20:20 . . . . . . . . . . . . . . . . . . . . . . . . 18
21:7 . . . . . . . . . . . . . . . . . . . . 102, 103
22:13-20 . . . . . . . . . . . . . . . . . . . . . 88
23:4 . . . . . . . . . . . . . . . . . . . . . . . . 102
23:7 . . . . . . . . . . . . . . . . . . . . . . . . . 98
23:13 . . . . . . . . . . 109, 112, 118, 120
23:29 . . . . . . . . . . . . . . . . . . . . . . . . 22
24:2 . . . . . . . . . . . 117, 118, 121, 123
24:14 . . . . . . . . . . . . . . . . . . . . . . . . 23
25:4-10 . . . . . . . . . . . . . . . . . . . . . . 23
25:12 . . . . . . . . . . . . . . . . . . . . . . . . 24
25:22 . . . . . . . . . . . . . . . . . . . . . . . . 24
25:25 . . . . . . . . . . . . . . . . . . . . . . . . 24
25:27-30 . . . . . . . . . . . . . . . . . . . . . 25

# 1 Chronicles

. . . . . . . . . . . . . . . . . . . . . . . . . . . . 72
1:13 . . . . . . . . . . . . . . . . . . . . . . . . . 53
7:8 . . . . . . . . . . . . . . . . . . . . . . . . . 109
26:13 . . . . . . . . . . . . . . . . . . . . . . . . . 5

# 2 Chronicles

. . . . . . . . . . . . . . . . . . . . . . . . . . . . 72
1:17 . . . . . . . . . . . . . . . . . . . . . . . . . 54
2:13 . . . . . . . . . . . . . . . . . . . . . . . . 112
12:1-12 . . . . . . . . . . . . . . . . . . . . . . 40
14:8-14 . . . . . . . . . . . . . . . . . . . . . . 40
20:1-30 . . . . . . . . . . . . . . . . . . . . . 121
28:17 . . . . . . . . . . . . . . . . . . . . . . . 123
36:23 . . . . . . . . . . . . . . . . . . . . . . . . 65

# Ezra

1–2 . . . . . . . . . . . . . . . . . . . . . . . . . 65
1:2-4 . . . . . . . . . . . . . . . . . . . . . . . . 65
1:5-6 . . . . . . . . . . . . . . . . . . . . . . . . 65
1:7 . . . . . . . . . . . . . . . . . . . . . . . . . . 65
1:8 . . . . . . . . . . . . . . . . . . . . . . . . . . 65
2 . . . . . . . . . . . . . . . . . . . . . . . . . . . 65
2:63 . . . . . . . . . . . . . . . . . . . . . . . . . . 6
2:64 . . . . . . . . . . . . . . . . . . . . . . . . . 65
4:8–6:18 . . . . . . . . . . . . . . . . . . . . 117
5:14-16 . . . . . . . . . . . . . . . . . . . . . . 66
6:3-5 . . . . . . . . . . . . . . . . . . . . . 64–65
7 . . . . . . . . . . . . . . . . . . . . . . . . . . . 69
7:7 . . . . . . . . . . . . . . . . . . . . . . . . . . 69
7:12-26 . . . . . . . . . . . . . . . . . 69, 117
9:1-2 . . . . . . . . . . . . . . . . . . . 119, 121

# Nehemiah

2:1 . . . . . . . . . . . . . . . . . . . . . . . . . . 67

2:3 . . . . . . . . . . . . . . . . . . . . . . . . 68
2:5 . . . . . . . . . . . . . . . . . . . . . . . . 68
2:10 . . . . . . . . . . . . . . . . . . . . . . . 119
2:19 . . . . . . . . . . . . . . . 70, 119, 124
2:63 . . . . . . . . . . . . . . . . . . . . . . . . 6
3:8 . . . . . . . . . . . . . . . . . . . . . . . . 18
3:33-42 [Eng 4:1-9] . . . . . . . . . . . 69
3:35 [Eng 4:3] . . . . . . . . . . . . . . 119
4:1 [Eng v. 7] . . . . . . . . . . . . . . . 119
4:13-23 . . . . . . . . . . . . . . . . . . . . 69
5 . . . . . . . . . . . . . . . . . . . . . . . . . 68
6:1 . . . . . . . . . . . . . . . . . . . . . . . 124
6:2 . . . . . . . . . . . . . . . . . . . . . . . 124
6:6 . . . . . . . . . . . . . . . . . . . . . . . 124
6:6-7 . . . . . . . . . . . . . . . . . . . . . . 68
7 . . . . . . . . . . . . . . . . . . . . . . . . . 65
7:6-73 . . . . . . . . . . . . . . . . . . . . . 65
7:65 . . . . . . . . . . . . . . . . . . . . . . . 6
8:1-3 . . . . . . . . . . . . . . . . . . . . . . 69
8:8 . . . . . . . . . . . . . . . . . . . . . . . 117
10:20 . . . . . . . . . . . . . . . . . . . . . 109
12:23 . . . . . . . . . . . . . . . . . . . . . . 70
13:4-5 . . . . . . . . . . . . . . . . . . . . 119
13:15-21 . . . . . . . . . . . . . . . . . . . 69
13:23 . . . . . . . . . . . . . . . . 119, 121
13:23-29 . . . . . . . . . . . . . . . . . . . 69

## Tobit

1:22 . . . . . . . . . . . . . . . . . . . . . . . 70

## Esther

. . . . . . . . . . . . . . . . . . . . . . . . . . 72

## 1 Maccabees

. . . . . . . . . . . . . . . . . . . . . . . . . . 81

## 2 Maccabees

. . . . . . . . . . . . . . . . . . . . . . . . . . 81
3 . . . . . . . . . . . . . . . . . . . . . . . . . 79

## Job

. . . . . . . . . . . . 13, 14, 46, 47, 72, 100
1:6 . . . . . . . . . . . . . . . . . . . . . . . . 14
1:7 . . . . . . . . . . . . . . . . . . . . . . . . 72
2:1 . . . . . . . . . . . . . . . . . . . . . 14, 72
3:8 . . . . . . . . . . . . . . . . . . . . . . . 107
7:12 . . . . . . . . . . . . . . . . . . . . . . 106
9:13 . . . . . . . . . . . . . . . . . . . . . . 106
9:33 . . . . . . . . . . . . . . . . . . . . . . . 4
12:9 . . . . . . . . . . . . . . . . . . . . . . 100
19:25 . . . . . . . . . . . . . . . . . . . . . . 4
26:5 . . . . . . . . . . . . . . . . . . . . . . 107
26:12 . . . . . . . . . . . . . . . . . . . . . 106
26:13 . . . . . . . . . . . . . . . . . . . . . 106
31 . . . . . . . . . . . . . . . . . . . . . . . . 47
31:1 . . . . . . . . . . . . . . . . . . . . . . 109
31:9 . . . . . . . . . . . . . . . . . . . . . . . 47
31:9-12 . . . . . . . . . . . . . . . . . . . . 109
31:13 . . . . . . . . . . . . . . . . . . . . . . 47
31:16 . . . . . . . . . . . . . . . . . . . . . . 47
31:18 . . . . . . . . . . . . . . . . . . . . . . 47
31:21 . . . . . . . . . . . . . . . . . . . . . . 47
31:24-25 . . . . . . . . . . . . . . . . . . . 47
38:8-11 . . . . . . . . . . . . . . . . . . . 107
40–41 . . . . . . . . . . . . . . . . . . . . . 106
41:18-21 . . . . . . . . . . . . . . . . . . . 106

## Psalms

18:10-12 [Eng vv. 9-11] . . . . . . . 105
29 . . . . . . . . . . . . . . . . . . . . . . . 105
29:3 . . . . . . . . . . . . . . . . . . 105, 106
29:4 . . . . . . . . . . . . . . . . . . . . . . 105
29:5 . . . . . . . . . . . . . . . . . . . . . . 105
29:7 . . . . . . . . . . . . . . . . . . . . . . 105
29:8 . . . . . . . . . . . . . . . . . . . . . . 105
29:9 . . . . . . . . . . . . . . . . . . . . . . 105
29:10 . . . . . . . . . . . . . . . . . 105, 106
33:7 . . . . . . . . . . . . . . . . . . . . . . 107
36:7 [Eng v. 6] . . . . . . . . . . . . . . 100
48:3 [Eng v. 2] . . . . . . . . . . . . 96, 97

48:12 [Eng v. 11] . . . . . . . . . . . . . . 96
49:14 . . . . . . . . . . . . . . . . . . . . . . 107
68:5 [Eng v. 4] . . . . . . . . . . . . . . . 105
68:9 [Eng v. 8] . . . . . . . . . . . . . . . 105
68:18 [Eng v. 17] . . . . . . . . 105, 124
68:24 [Eng v. 23] . . . . . . . . . . . . . 109
68:34 [Eng v. 33] . . . . . . . . . . . . . 105
73:1 . . . . . . . . . . . . . . . . . . . . . . . . 95
74:12-17 . . . . . . . . . . . . . . . . . . . 106
74:13 . . . . . . . . . . . . . . . . . . . . . . 106
74:14 . . . . . . . . . . . . . . . . . . . . . . 106
75:10 [Eng v. 9] . . . . . . . . . . 99–100
77:17-21 [Eng vv. 16-20] . . . . . . 106
87:4 . . . . . . . . . . . . . . . . . . . . . . . 106
88:10 . . . . . . . . . . . . . . . . . . . . . . 107
89:10-13 [Eng vv. 9-12] . . . . . . . 106
89:11 [Eng v. 10] . . . . . . . . . . . . . 106
91:1 . . . . . . . . . . . . . . . . . . . . . . . 100
93 . . . . . . . . . . . . . . . . . . . . . . . . 106
104 . . . . . . . . . . . . . . . . . . . . . 34–36
104:3 . . . . . . . . . . . . . . . . . . . . . . 105
104:5-9 . . . . . . . . . . . . . . . . . . . . 107
104:10 . . . . . . . . . . . . . . . . . . . . . . 35
104:11 . . . . . . . . . . . . . . . . . . . . . . 35
104:12 . . . . . . . . . . . . . . . . . . . . . . 35
104:13 . . . . . . . . . . . . . . . . . . . . . . 35
104:14 . . . . . . . . . . . . . . . . . . . . . . 35
104:20 . . . . . . . . . . . . . . . . . . . . . . 34
104:21 . . . . . . . . . . . . . . . . . . . . . . 34
104:22 . . . . . . . . . . . . . . . . . . . . . . 35
104:23 . . . . . . . . . . . . . . . . . . . . . . 35
104:24 . . . . . . . . . . . . . . . . . . . . . . 35
104:25-26 . . . . . . . . . . . . . . . . . . . 35
104:27 . . . . . . . . . . . . . . . . . . . . . . 35
104:29-30 . . . . . . . . . . . . . . . . . . . 35
106:9 . . . . . . . . . . . . . . . . . . . . . . 106
106:28 . . . . . . . . . . . . . . . . . . . . . 120
114:3 . . . . . . . . . . . . . . . . . . . . . . 106
114:5 . . . . . . . . . . . . . . . . . . . . . . 106
132:2 . . . . . . . . . . . . . . . . . . . . . . 101
132:5 . . . . . . . . . . . . . . . . . . . . . . 101
137 . . . . . . . . . . . . . . . . . . . . . . . . 23
137:4 . . . . . . . . . . . . . . . . . . . . . . . 23

137:7 . . . . . . . . . . . . . . . . . . . . . . 123
141:7 . . . . . . . . . . . . . . . . . . . . . . 107

# Proverbs

. . . . . . . . . . . . . . . . . . . . . . . . . . . 46
1:8 . . . . . . . . . . . . . . . . . . . . . . 3, 41
1:8-19 . . . . . . . . . . . . . . . . . . . . . 41
1:9 . . . . . . . . . . . . . . . . . . . . . . . . 41
1:10 . . . . . . . . . . . . . . . . . . . . . . . . 3
1:10-19 . . . . . . . . . . . . . . . . . . . . 41
1:12 . . . . . . . . . . . . . . . . . . . . . . 107
1:15 . . . . . . . . . . . . . . . . . . . . . . . . 3
2 . . . . . . . . . . . . . . . . . . . . . . . . . 42
2:1 . . . . . . . . . . . . . . . . . . . . . . 3, 41
2:1-22 . . . . . . . . . . . . . . . . . . . . . 41
2:2-4 . . . . . . . . . . . . . . . . . . . . . . 41
2:5-8 . . . . . . . . . . . . . . . . . . . . . . 41
2:9-11 . . . . . . . . . . . . . . . . . . . . . 41
2:12-15 . . . . . . . . . . . . . . . . . . . . 41
2:16-19 . . . . . . . . . . . . . . . . . . . . 41
2:18 . . . . . . . . . . . . . . . . . . . . . . 107
2:20-22 . . . . . . . . . . . . . . . . . . . . 41
3:1 . . . . . . . . . . . . . . . . . . . . . . . . . 3
3:1-12 . . . . . . . . . . . . . . . . . . . . . 42
3:11 . . . . . . . . . . . . . . . . . . . . . . . . 3
3:21 . . . . . . . . . . . . . . . . . . . . . . . . 3
3:21-35 . . . . . . . . . . . . . . . . . . . . 42
4:1 . . . . . . . . . . . . . . . . . . . . . . . . . 3
4:1-9 . . . . . . . . . . . . . . . . . . . . . . 42
4:10 . . . . . . . . . . . . . . . . . . . . . . . . 3
4:10-19 . . . . . . . . . . . . . . . . . . . . 42
4:20-27 . . . . . . . . . . . . . . . . . . . . 42
5:1 . . . . . . . . . . . . . . . . . . . . . . . . . 3
5:1-23 . . . . . . . . . . . . . . . . . . . . . 42
5:3-6 . . . . . . . . . . . . . . . . . . . . . . 43
5:7 . . . . . . . . . . . . . . . . . . . . . . . . . 3
6:1 . . . . . . . . . . . . . . . . . . . . . . . . . 3
6:3 . . . . . . . . . . . . . . . . . . . . . . . . . 3
6:20 . . . . . . . . . . . . . . . . . . . . . . . . 3
6:20-35 . . . . . . . . . . . . . . . . . . . . 42
6:24-25 . . . . . . . . . . . . . . . . . . . . 43

7:1 . . . . . . . . . . . . . . . . . . . . . . . . . . . 3
7:1-27 . . . . . . . . . . . . . . . . . . . . . . . 42
7:13 . . . . . . . . . . . . . . . . . . . . . . . . . 43
7:16-17 . . . . . . . . . . . . . . . . . . . . . . 43
8:22-31 . . . . . . . . . . . . . . . . . . . . . . 71
8:27-29 . . . . . . . . . . . . . . . . . . . . . 107
13:24 . . . . . . . . . . . . . . . . . . . . . . . . 71
19:18 . . . . . . . . . . . . . . . . . . . . . . . . 71
22:17 . . . . . . . . . . . . . . . . . . . . . . . . 45
22:17-18 . . . . . . . . . . . . . . . . . . . . . 44
22:17–24:22 . . . . . . . . . . . . . . . . . 43
22:20 . . . . . . . . . . . . . . . . . . . . . . . . 43
22:22 . . . . . . . . . . . . . . . . . . . . 44, 45
22:24 . . . . . . . . . . . . . . . . . . . . . . . . 44
22:29 . . . . . . . . . . . . . . . . . . . . . . . . 44
23:1 . . . . . . . . . . . . . . . . . . . . . . . . . 44
23:4 . . . . . . . . . . . . . . . . . . . . . . . . . 45
23:10 . . . . . . . . . . . . . . . . . . . . . . . . 45
23:11 . . . . . . . . . . . . . . . . . . . . . . . . 45
23:13-14 . . . . . . . . . . . . . . . . . . . . . 71
23:19 . . . . . . . . . . . . . . . . . . . . . . . . . 3
23:25 . . . . . . . . . . . . . . . . . . . . . . . . . 3
23:26 . . . . . . . . . . . . . . . . . . . . . . . . . 3
24:13 . . . . . . . . . . . . . . . . . . . . . . . . . 3
24:21 . . . . . . . . . . . . . . . . . . . . . . . . . 3
25:21-22 . . . . . . . . . . . . . . . . . . . . . 95
27:11 . . . . . . . . . . . . . . . . . . . . . . . . . 3
30:15-16 . . . . . . . . . . . . . . . . . . . . . 46
30:18-19 . . . . . . . . . . . . . . . . . . . . . 46
30:21-28 . . . . . . . . . . . . . . . . . . . . . 46
30:29-31 . . . . . . . . . . . . . . . . . . . . . 46

## Qoheleth (Ecclesiastes)

 . . . . . . . . . . . 12, 27, 46, 47, 72, 77
1:4 . . . . . . . . . . . . . . . . . . . . . . . . . 77
1:4-7 . . . . . . . . . . . . . . . . . . . . . . . . 77
1:5 . . . . . . . . . . . . . . . . . . . . . . . . . 78
1:6 . . . . . . . . . . . . . . . . . . . . . . . . . 77
1:7 . . . . . . . . . . . . . . . . . . . . . . . . . 78
1:9 . . . . . . . . . . . . . . . . . . . . . . . . . 78
2:5 . . . . . . . . . . . . . . . . . . . . . . . . . 72

2:24 . . . . . . . . . . . . . . . . . . . 13, 47, 78
3:1 . . . . . . . . . . . . . . . . . . . . . . . . . 77
3:1-9 . . . . . . . . . . . . . . . . . . . . . 27, 77
3:5 . . . . . . . . . . . . . . . . . . . . . . . . . 27
3:12-13 . . . . . . . . . . . . . . . . 13, 47, 78
3:21 . . . . . . . . . . . . . . . . . . . . . . . . 78
3:22 . . . . . . . . . . . . . . . . . . . 13, 47, 78
4:9-12 . . . . . . . . . . . . . . . . . . . . . . 12
5:8 . . . . . . . . . . . . . . . . . . . . . . . . . 72
5:17-18 . . . . . . . . . . . . . . . . 13, 47, 78
7:16-18 . . . . . . . . . . . . . . . . . . . . . 78
7:26-28 . . . . . . . . . . . . . . . . . . . . . 43
7:27 . . . . . . . . . . . . . . . . . . . . . . . . 78
8:11 . . . . . . . . . . . . . . . . . . . . . . . . 72
8:15 . . . . . . . . . . . . . . . . . . . 13, 47, 78
9:7-9 . . . . . . . . . . . . . . . . . . . . . . . 13
11:9 . . . . . . . . . . . . . . . . . . . 13, 47, 78

## Song of Songs

 . . . . . . . . . . . . . . . . . . . . . . 108, 109
4:1-6 . . . . . . . . . . . . . . . . . . . . . . . 49
5:10-15 . . . . . . . . . . . . . . . . . . . . . 49
6:4-7 . . . . . . . . . . . . . . . . . . . . . . . 49
7:1-5 . . . . . . . . . . . . . . . . . . . . . . . 28
7:1-9 . . . . . . . . . . . . . . . . . . . . . . . 49

## Sirach

 . . . . . . . . . . . . . . . . . . . . . . . . . . . 46
38:24-39:11 . . . . . . . . . . . . . . . . . 46

## Isaiah

1:24 . . . . . . . . . . . . . . . . . . . . . . . 101
4:2 . . . . . . . . . . . . . . . . . . . . . . . . . 67
5:14 . . . . . . . . . . . . . . . . . . . . . . . 107
6:9-10 . . . . . . . . . . . . . . . . . . . . . . 14
7 . . . . . . . . . . . . . . . . . . . . . . . . . 117
7–8 . . . . . . . . . . . . . . . . . . . . . . . . 17
11:1 . . . . . . . . . . . . . . . . . . . . . . . . 67
14:9 . . . . . . . . . . . . . . . . . . . 107, 108

14:12-15 . . . . . . . . . . . . . . . . . . . 107
17:7-8 . . . . . . . . . . . . . . . . . . . . . 104
19:1 . . . . . . . . . . . . . . . . . . . . . . . 105
22:10 . . . . . . . . . . . . . . . . . . . . . . 18
25:7 [Eng v. 8] . . . . . . . . . . . . . 107
26:14 . . . . . . . . . . . . . . . . . . . . . 107
27:1 . . . . . . . . . . . . . . . . . . . . . . 106
27:9 . . . . . . . . . . . . . . . . . . . . . . 104
28:15 . . . . . . . . . . . . . . . . . . . . . 107
28:18 . . . . . . . . . . . . . . . . . . . . . 107
29:4 . . . . . . . . . . . . . . . . . . . . . . . 57
30:7 . . . . . . . . . . . . . . . . . . . . . . 106
34 . . . . . . . . . . . . . . . . . . . . . . . 123
34:14 . . . . . . . . . . . . . . . . . . . . . . 15
37:2-7 . . . . . . . . . . . . . . . . . . . . . 88
39:1 . . . . . . . . . . . . . . . . . . . . . . . 18
40–55 . . . . . . . . . . . . . . . . . . . . . 28
40:18-20 . . . . . . . . . . . . . . . . . . . 28
40:25-26 . . . . . . . . . . . . . . . . . . . 28
41:1-4 . . . . . . . . . . . . . . . . . . . . . 28
41:26-29 . . . . . . . . . . . . . . . . . . . 28
44:6-7 . . . . . . . . . . . . . . . . . . . . . 28
45:1 . . . . . . . . . . . . . . . . . . . . . . . 65
45:7 . . . . . . . . . . . . . . . . . . . . . . . 73
45:21-22 . . . . . . . . . . . . . . . . . . . 29
49:26 . . . . . . . . . . . . . . . . . . . . . 101
51:9-10 . . . . . . . . . . . . . . . . . . . 106
60:16 . . . . . . . . . . . . . . . . . . . . . 101
63:3-6 . . . . . . . . . . . . . . . . . . . . 109

23:9 . . . . . . . . . . . . . . . . . . . . 39, 87
23:37 . . . . . . . . . . . . . . . . . . . . . . 88
26:24 . . . . . . . . . . . . . . . . . . . . . . 24
27:3 . . . . . . . . . . . . . . . . . . . . . . 123
29:26 . . . . . . . . . . . . . . . . . . . . . . 88
34:18-19 . . . . . . . . . . . . . . . . . . . 89
37:3-10 . . . . . . . . . . . . . . . . . . . . 88
39:3 . . . . . . . . . . . . . . . . . . . . . . . 26
39:10 . . . . . . . . . . . . . . . . . . . . . . 24
40:7-12 . . . . . . . . . . . . . . . . . . . . 25
40:11-12 . . . . . . . . . . . . . . . . . . . 24
40:14 . . . . . . . . . . . . . . . . . . . . . . 24
40:13–41:15 . . . . . . . . . . . . . . . 119
43 . . . . . . . . . . . . . . . . . . . . . . . . 24
44:1 . . . . . . . . . . . . . . . . . . . . . . . 25
44:17 . . . . . . . . . . . . . . . . . . . . . . 28
44:17-19 . . . . . . . . . . . . . . . . 28, 110
44:25 . . . . . . . . . . . . . . . . . . . 28, 110
44:29 . . . . . . . . . . . . . . . . . . . . . 110
49:1 . . . . . . . . . . . . . . . . . . . . . . 119
51:34 . . . . . . . . . . . . . . . . . . . . . 106
52:28 . . . . . . . . . . . . . . . . . . . . . . 23
52:30 . . . . . . . . . . . . . . . . . . . . . . 23
52:31 . . . . . . . . . . . . . . . . . . . . . . 25

## Lamentations

. . . . . . . . . . . . . . . . . . . . . . . 5, 25
4:21-22 . . . . . . . . . . . . . . . . . . . 123

## Jeremiah

. . . . . . . . . . . . . . . . . . . . . . . . . . 5
1:1 . . . . . . . . . . . . . . . . . . . . . . . 109
4:13 . . . . . . . . . . . . . . . . . . . . . . 105
5:22 . . . . . . . . . . . . . . . . . . . . . . 107
7:18 . . . . . . . . . . . . . . . . . . . 28, 110
10:11 . . . . . . . . . . . . . . . . . . . . . 117
17:2 . . . . . . . . . . . . . . . . . . . . . . 104
20:9 . . . . . . . . . . . . . . . . . . . . 39, 87
21:1-7 . . . . . . . . . . . . . . . . . . . . . 88
23:5 . . . . . . . . . . . . . . . . . . . . . . . 67

## Ezekiel

. . . . . . . . . . . . . . . . . . . . . . . . . . 5
1 . . . . . . . . . . . . . . . . . . . . . . . . . 16
1:1 . . . . . . . . . . . . . . . . . . . . . . . . 23
8:3 . . . . . . . . . . . . . . . . . . . . . . . . 87
8:14 . . . . . . . . . . . . . . . . . . . . . . . 15
10:18-19 . . . . . . . . . . . . . . . . . . . 16
16:3 . . . . . . . . . . . . . . . . . . . . . . . 54
16:45 . . . . . . . . . . . . . . . . . . . . . . 54
21 . . . . . . . . . . . . . . . . . . . . . . . . 27
24–32 . . . . . . . . . . . . . . . . . . . . . 27

25:12 . . . . . . . . . . . . . . . . . . . . . . 123
29:3 . . . . . . . . . . . . . . . . . . . . . . . 106
32:2 . . . . . . . . . . . . . . . . . . . . . . . 106
35:3 . . . . . . . . . . . . . . . . . . . . . . . 123
35:15 . . . . . . . . . . . . . . . . . . . . . . 123
47:16 . . . . . . . . . . . . . . . . . . . . . . . 54

## Daniel

. . . . . . . . . . . . . . . . . . . . . . . 76, 81
2:4b–7:28 . . . . . . . . . . . . . . . . . . 117
4:32 . . . . . . . . . . . . . . . . . . . . . . . . 26
5 . . . . . . . . . . . . . . . . . . . . . . . . . . 26
7–12 . . . . . . . . . . . . . . . . . 73, 81, 82
7:2-8 . . . . . . . . . . . . . . . . . . . . . . . 82
7:9 . . . . . . . . . . . . . . . . . . . . . . . . . 98
7:13 . . . . . . . . . . . . . . . . . . . . 98, 106
7:23-24 . . . . . . . . . . . . . . . . . . . . . 82
7:25 . . . . . . . . . . . . . . . . . . . . . . . . 82
7:26-27 . . . . . . . . . . . . . . . . . . . . . 83
8 . . . . . . . . . . . . . . . . . . . . . . . . . . 83
8:3 . . . . . . . . . . . . . . . . . . . . . . . . . 83
8:4 . . . . . . . . . . . . . . . . . . . . . . . . . 83
8:5 . . . . . . . . . . . . . . . . . . . . . . . . . 83
8:6-8 . . . . . . . . . . . . . . . . . . . . . . . 83
8:9-12 . . . . . . . . . . . . . . . . . . . . . . 83
8:13 . . . . . . . . . . . . . . . . . . . . . . . . 83
8:23-25 . . . . . . . . . . . . . . . . . . . . . 83
9 . . . . . . . . . . . . . . . . . . . . . . . . . . 83
9:26 . . . . . . . . . . . . . . . . . . . . . . . . 83
9:27 . . . . . . . . . . . . . . . . . . . . . . . . 83
10:2-9 . . . . . . . . . . . . . . . . . . . . . . 83
11 . . . . . . . . . . . . . . . . . . . . . . . . . 83
11:5 . . . . . . . . . . . . . . . . . . . . . . . . 83
11:6-9 . . . . . . . . . . . . . . . . . . . . . . 84
11:10-19 . . . . . . . . . . . . . . . . . . . . 84
11:20 . . . . . . . . . . . . . . . . . . . . . . . 84
11:21-39 . . . . . . . . . . . . . . . . . . . . 84
11:30 . . . . . . . . . . . . . . . . . . . . . . . 84
12 . . . . . . . . . . . . . . . . . . . . . . . . . 84
12:7 . . . . . . . . . . . . . . . . . . . . . . . . 84
12:11 . . . . . . . . . . . . . . . . . . . . . . . 84

## Hosea

2:2-3 . . . . . . . . . . . . . . . . . . . 91, 94
4:14 . . . . . . . . . . . . . . . . . . . . . . . . 98
4:17-19 . . . . . . . . . . . . . . . . . . . . 109
9:7 . . . . . . . . . . . . . . . . . . . . . . . . . 88
9:10 . . . . . . . . . . . . . . . . . . . . . . . 120

## Joel

4:19 [Eng 3:19] . . . . . . . . . . . . . 123

## Amos

1–2 . . . . . . . . . . . . . . . . . . . . . . . . 96
1:1 . . . . . . . . . . . . . . . . . . . . . . . . . 96
5:26 . . . . . . . . . . . . . . . . . . . . . . . . 15
7:10-14 . . . . . . . . . . . . . . . . . . . . . 87

## Obadiah

3 . . . . . . . . . . . . . . . . . . . . . . . . . 122
11-14 . . . . . . . . . . . . . . . . . . . . . . 123

## Micah

3:7 . . . . . . . . . . . . . . . . . . . . . . . . . 88
5:13 [Eng v. 14] . . . . . . . . . . . . . 104
6:5 . . . . . . . . . . . . . . . . . . . . . . . . . 88

## Nahum

1:3 . . . . . . . . . . . . . . . . . . . . . . . . 105

## Habakkuk

2:5 . . . . . . . . . . . . . . . . . . . . . . . . 107
3:3 . . . . . . . . . . . . . . . . . . . . . . . . 125
3:8 . . . . . . . . . . . . . . . . . . . . . . . . 106
3:10 . . . . . . . . . . . . . . . . . . . . . . . 106
3:15 . . . . . . . . . . . . . . . . . . . . . . . 106

## Haggai

........................ 67, 72
1:1 ........................ 67
2:1 ........................ 67
2:20 ........................ 67
2:21-23 .................... 67

3 ........................... 72
3:8 ......................... 67
4:6-10 ...................... 67
4:8 ......................... 67
5:5-11 ...................... 56
6:12 ........................ 67

## Zechariah

........................ 67, 72

## Malachi

1:2-5 ...................... 123

# Other Texts and Inscriptions

## Akkadian

Epic of Atrahasis .......... 9, 26
Laws of Eshnunna ........ 10–11

## Aramean

Tel Dan Stele ........... 116, 121

## Assyrian

Black Obelisk (Shalmaneser III)  16
Jerusalem Prism .............. 18
Lachish Relief ................ 19
Legend of Sargon, The ......... 4
Sennacherib's Prism ....... 18–19
Taylor Prism ................. 18
Vassal Treaties .............. 60

## Babylonian

Babylonian Theodicy, The ..... 14
Code of Hammurabi  11, 12, 26, 55
Dialogue of Pessimism ........ 27
Enuma Elish ............. 8, 9, 26

Epic of Gilgamesh   9–10, 12, 13, 26
Erra and Ishum ............. 27
I Will Praise the Lord of
  Wisdom ............... 13–14
*Ludlul bēl nēmeqi* ........... 13–14

## Egyptian

Book of the Dead ............ 47
Dialogue of a Man with His
  Soul ...................... 47
Dispute over Suicide, The ..... 47
el-Amarna Letters ........ 36, 111
Great Hymn to the Aten .... 34–36
In Praise of Learned Scribes  ... 46
Instruction of a Man for His
  Son ..................... 46
Instruction of Amenemope  ... 43–
                          45, 46
Instruction of Ani .......... 43
Instruction of Kagemni ...... 43
Instruction of Khety ........ 46
Instruction of King
  Amenemhet .............. 43
Instruction of King Merikare ... 43
Instruction of Onkhsheshonqy  45

Instruction of Prince Hardjedef  43
Instruction of Ptahhotep  . . . 42–43
Karnak Reliefs  . . . . . . . . . 38–39, 40
Lamentations of
  Khakheperre-sonbe . . . . . . . . . 47
Love Songs . . . . . . . . . . . . . . . . . 49
Merneptah's Stele  . . . . . . 37, 38, 39
Papyrus Anastasi  . . . . . . . . . . . 46
Papyrus Insinger . . . . . . . . . . . . 45
Papyrus Sallier . . . . . . . . . . . . . . 46
Report of Wen-amun  . . . . . . . . . 39
Song of the Harper  . . . . . . . . . . . 47
Tale of the Eloquent Peasant  46–47
Tale of Sinuhe  . . . . . . . . . . . . . . 48
Tale of Two Brothers  . . . . . . 48, 61

## Greek

Herodotus, Histories 2.141 . . 19–20

## Hittite

Elkunirša Myth  . . . . . . . . 60–61, 99
Hittite Law Code . . . . . . . . . . . . . 55
Legend of Zalpa  . . . . . . . . . . . . . 57
Vassal Treaties . . . . . . 57–58, 59, 60

## Israelite/Jewish

Elephantine Texts  . . . . . . . . . 70–71
Lachish Letters . . . . . . . . . . . . . . 24

Proverbs of Ahiqar  . . . . 70, 71, 117

## Moabite

Deir Alla Balaam
  Inscription  . . . . . . . . . . . 119–20
Mesha Stele  . . . . . . . . . . . . 120–21
Moabite Stone  . . . . . . . . . . . . . 120

## Persian

Behistun Inscription . . . 66, 70, 117
Cyrus Cylinder  . . . . . . . . . . . 64, 65

## Sumerian

Curse of Agade, The . . . . . . . . . . . 5
Enmerkar and the Lord of Aratta  4
Eridu Genesis, The  . . . . . . . . . . . 4
King List . . . . . . . . . . . . . . . . . . . 4
Lament for Eridu, The  . . . . . . . . . 5
Lament for Nippur, The . . . . . . . . 5
Lament for Sumer and Ur, The . . 5
Lament for Ur, The  . . . . . . . . . . . 5
Lament for Uruk, The . . . . . . . . . . 5
Man and His God, A . . . . . . . . . . . 3

## Other

1 Esdras 4:45  . . . . . . . . . . . . . . 123
Zakkur Stele . . . . . . . . . . . . 116–17

# Index of Names

## Deities/ Mythological Beings

Adad . . . . . . . . . . . . . . . . . . . . . 28
Ahriman . . . . . . . . . . . . . . . . . . . 73
Ahura Mazda . . . . . . . . . . . . . . . 73
Amun . . . . . . . . . . . . . . . . . . . 39, 40
Amun-Re . . . . . . . . . . . . . . . 33, 34
Anat . . . . . . . . 61, 70, 104, 106, 108,
109, 110
Anat-Bethel . . . . . . . . . . . . . . . . 70
Anat-Yahu . . . . . . . . . . . . . . . . . 70
Angra Mainyu . . . . . . . . . . . . . . 73
Asherah . . . . . . . . 60, 99, 101–4, 115
Ashertu . . . . . . . . . . . . . . . . . 60, 61
Ashtar . . . . . . . . . . . . . . . . . . . . . 86
Ashtar-Chemosh . . . . . . . . . . . . 120
Astarte . . . . . . . 28, 109–10, 112, 115
Aten . . . . . . . . . . . . . . . . . . 33, 34, 35
Athirat . . . . . . . . . . . . . . . . . 60, 101
Athtar . . . . . . . . . . . . . . . . . . . . . 107
Athtart . . . . . . . . . . . . . . . . . . . . . 109
Azazel . . . . . . . . . . . . . . . . . . 15, 56

Ba'al . . . . . 39, 61, 86, 87, 89, 93, 97,
99, 102, 103, 104–7, 108,
109, 112, 114, 120, 124
Ba'al-zebub . . . . . . . . . . . . . . . . 114
Ba'al-zebul . . . . . . . . . . . . . . . . 114
Behemoth . . . . . . . . . . . . . . . . . 106
Bethel . . . . . . . . . . . . . . . . . . . . . 70

Chemosh . . . . . . . . . . . . . . . . . . 120

Dagon . . . . . . . . . . . . . . 86, 87, 114
Dawn . . . . . . . . . . . . . . . . . 107, 110
Death . . . . . . . . . . . . . 104, 107, 108
Dumuzi . . . . . . . . . . . . . . . . . . . 15
Dusk . . . . . . . . . . . . . . . . . . . . . 110

Ea . . . . . . . . . . . . . . . . . . . . . . . . 4, 9
El . . . . . . . . . 29, 60, 61, 98–101, 104,
106, 108, 110, 125
El Shaddai . . . . . . . . . . . . . 100, 101
Elkunirša . . . . . . . . . . . . . . . . 60, 99
Enki . . . . . . . . . . . . . . . . . . . . . . 4, 9
Enlil . . . . . . . . . . . . . . . . . . . . . . 5, 9

Gabriel . . . . . . . . . . . . . . . . . . . . 83

140

Hadad . . . . . . . . . . . . . . . . . . 86, 87
Hathor . . . . . . . . . . . . . . . . . 48, 125
Hebat . . . . . . . . . . . . . . . . . . . . . . 56

Ishtar . . . . . 4, 20, 28, 29, 86, 87, 110

Kaiwan . . . . . . . . . . . . . . . . . . . . 15
Khnum . . . . . . . . . . . . . . . . . . . . 70
Kingu . . . . . . . . . . . . . . . . . . . . . 9

Lady Wisdom . . . . . . . . . . . . . . 71
Leviathan . . . . . . . 35, 106, 107, 108
Lilith . . . . . . . . . . . . . . . . . . . . . 15
Litanu . . . . . . . . . . . . . . . . . . . 106
Lotan . . . . . . . . . . . . . . . . . . . . 106

Marduk . . . . . . . . 8, 14, 25, 26, 28,
29, 64, 87
Melqart . . . . . . . . . . . . . . 104, 112
Milcom . . . . . . . . . . . . . . . . . . 118
Molech . . . . . . . . . . . . . . . . . . 118
Mot . . . . . . . . . . . . . . 104, 107, 108

Ninurta . . . . . . . . . . . . . . . . . . . 15

Queen of Heaven . . . . . . . . . 28, 110

Rahab . . . . . . . . . . . . . . . . . . . 106
Rephaim . . . . . . . . . . . . 107–8, 114
Resheph . . . . . . . . . . . . . . . . . . 86

Sakkuth . . . . . . . . . . . . . . . . . . . 15
śāṭān, the . . . . . . . . . . . . . . . . . . 72
Satan . . . . . . . . . . . . . . . . . . . . . 73
Sea . . . . . 89, 104, 105, 106, 107, 108
Shaddai . . . . . . . . 100, 101, 119, 120
Shaddayin . . . . . . . . . . . . . . . . 120
Shamash . . . . . . . . . . . . . . . . 28, 87
Shapash . . . . . . . . . . . . . . . . . . . 86
Sheger . . . . . . . . . . . . . . . . . . . . 89
Sin . . . . . . . . . . . . . . . . . . . . 26, 28

Tammuz . . . . . . . . . . . . . . . . . . . 15

Tiamat . . . . . . . . . . . . . . . . . . 8, 9, 89

Venus . . . . . . . . . . . . . . . . . . . . 107

Yahu . . . . . . . . . . . . . . . . . . . . . . 70
Yahweh . . 4, 5, 8, 10, 25, 27, 28, 29,
34, 35, 58, 59, 60, 65, 70, 73, 86,
88, 89, 97–109, 112, 120, 124–25
Yam . . . . . . . . . . . . . . . . . . 104, 106

Zeus . . . . . . . . . . . . . . . . . . . . 80, 83

## Groups

ʿapiru . . . . . . . . . . . . . . . . . . 36, 122
Akkadians . . . . . . . . . . . . . . . . 2–3
Ammonites . . . . . . 118–19, 121, 123
Amorites . . . . . . . . . . . 6, 31, 54, 85
Arabs . . . . . . . . . . . . . . . . . . . . . 17
Arameans . . 8, 16, 54, 115, 117, 123
Assyrians . . . . 16, 18, 19, 22, 23, 52,
53, 54, 63, 111, 114, 116, 117
Athenians . . . . . . . . . . . . . . . . . 68

Babylonians . . . . . . 7, 15, 22, 23, 24,
25, 63, 64, 114, 119

Canaanites . . . . . 39, 54, 97, 98, 110

Edomites . . . . . . . . . . . . 90, 122, 123
Egyptians . . . . 18, 20, 22, 31, 33, 34,
37, 38, 39, 52, 58, 69, 94, 97
Elamites . . . . . . . . . . . . . . . . . . 6, 7
Ethiopians . . . . . . . . . . . . . . . . . 18

Girgashites . . . . . . . . . . . . . . . . 54
Greeks . . . . . . . . 71, 79, 82, 110, 111
Gutians . . . . . . . . . . . . . . . . . . 3, 5

Hittites . . . . 7, 33, 37, 51, 52, 53, 54,
55, 56, 85, 90, 94
Hivites . . . . . . . . . . . . . . . . . . . . 54

Horites . . . . . . . . . . . . . . . . 90, 122
Hurrians . . . . . . . . . . . . 90, 94, 122
Hyksos . . . . . . . . . . . . 31, 32, 33, 43

Israel/Israelites . . . . . 3, 4, 5, 10, 13,
17, 26, 29, 32, 34, 36, 37, 38, 39,
54, 60, 102, 104, 111, 112, 113, 118,
119, 120, 121, 122, 123, 124, 125

Jebusites . . . . . . . . . . . . . . . . . . . 54
Judahites . . . . . . . . . . . . . . . 26, 28
Judeans . . . . . . . . . . . . . . . . 24, 79

Kassites . . . . . . . . . . . . . . . . . . . . 7
Kittim . . . . . . . . . . . . . . . . . . . . . 84

Levites . . . . . . . . . . . . . . . . . . . . 55
Libyans . . . . . . . . . . . . . . . . . . . 38

Maccabees . . . . . . . . . . . . . . . . . 81
Medes . . . . . . . . . . . . . . . . . . 64, 83
Moabites . . . . . . . 120, 121, 123, 124

Nabateans . . . . . . . . . . . . . . . . 124
Nubians . . . . . . . . . . . . . . . . . . . 32

Peleset . . . . . . . . . . . . . . 39, 53, 113
Perizzites . . . . . . . . . . . . . . . . . . 54
Persians . . . . . . . . . 1, 21, 26, 63, 64,
67, 68, 72, 83
Philistines . . . . . 20, 39, 53, 56, 110,
113–14, 118
Phoenicians . . . . . . . . . . . . 111, 112
Ptolemies . . . . . . . . . . 75, 76, 78, 83

*qdšm* . . . . . . . . . . . . . . . . . . . . 97–98

Romans . . . . . . . . . . . . . . . . . 79, 84

Samarians . . . . . . . . . . . . . . . . . 17
Samaritans . . . . . . . . . . . . . . . . . 17
Sea Peoples . . . . . . . . . 8, 38, 39, 53,
94, 111, 113

Seleucids . . . . . . . 75, 76, 79, 81, 83
Semites . . . . . . . . . . . 2, 3, 6, 31, 32,
111, 115, 117
Shasu . . . . . . . . . . . . . . . . . 122, 125
Sherden . . . . . . . . . . . . . . . . . . . 113
Stoics . . . . . . . . . . . . . . . . . . . . . 77
Sumerians . . . . . . . . . . . . . . 1, 2, 3

Tjekker . . . . . . . . . . . . . . . . . . . 113

Urartians . . . . . . . . . . . . . . . . . . 17

# Individuals

ʿAbdi-Ashirta . . . . . . . . . . . . . . . 36
ʿAbdi-Heba . . . . . . . . . . . . . . . . . 36
ʿAziru . . . . . . . . . . . . . . . . . . . . . 36
Aaron . . . . . . . . . . . . . . . . . 15, 124
Abdon . . . . . . . . . . . . . . . . . . . . . 57
Abraham . . . . . . . 53, 89, 90, 92, 101
Absalom . . . . . . . . . . . . . . . . . . 118
Achan . . . . . . . . . . . . . . . . . . . . . . 5
Achish . . . . . . . . . . . . . . . . . . . . 113
Adad-nirari III . . . . . . . . . . 117, 123
Adrammelech . . . . . . . . . . . . . . . 20
Ahab . . . 16, 112, 115, 116, 120, 121
Ahasuerus . . . . . . . . . . . . . . . . . 72
Ahaz . . . . . . . . . . . . . . . . . . 17, 117
Ahaziah . . . . . . . . . . . . . . . . . . . 116
Ahikam . . . . . . . . . . . . . . . . . . . . 24
Ahiqar . . . . . . . . . . . . . . . . . . 70, 71
Ahmose . . . . . . . . . . . . . . . . . . . . 32
Ahzai . . . . . . . . . . . . . . . . . . . . . 68
Akhenaten . . . . . . . . . 33, 34, 36, 52
Akki . . . . . . . . . . . . . . . . . . . . . . . . 4
Alexander the Great    71, 75, 82, 83
Amaziah . . . . . . . . . . . . . . . . 87, 123
Amel-Marduk . . . . . . . . . . . . . . 25
Amenemhet I . . . . . . . . . . . . . 43, 48
Amenhotep IV . . . . . . . . . . . . . . 33
Amos . . . . . . . . . . . . 16, 87, 96, 103
Anathoth . . . . . . . . . . . . . . . . 108–9

Ankhesenamun . . . . . . . . . . . . . . 52
Antiochus II . . . . . . . . . . . . . . 76, 83
Antiochus III . . . . . . . . . . 76, 78, 79
Antiochus IV . . . . . . . 79, 80, 81, 82,
83, 84
Antipater . . . . . . . . . . . . . . . . . . 81
Anubis . . . . . . . . . . . . . . . . . . . . . 48
Aqhat . . . . . . . . . . . . . . . . . . . . . 108
Arda-Mulissi . . . . . . . . . . . . . . . 20
Aristobulus II . . . . . . . . . . . . . . . 81
Aristotle . . . . . . . . . . . . . . . . . . . 78
Artaxerxes I . . . . . . . . . . . . . . 67, 68
Artaxerxes II . . . . . . . . . . . . . . . . 69
Asa . . . . . . . . . . . . . . . . 40, 102, 115
Ashurbanipal . . . . . 21, 28, 121, 123
Ashur-etil-ilani . . . . . . . . . . . . . 21
Ashurnasirpal II . . . . . . . . . . . . 111
Ashur-uballit I . . . . . . . . . . . . . 8, 90
Astyages . . . . . . . . . . . . . . . . 63, 64
Atrahasis . . . . . . . . . . . . . . . . . . . . 9
Ay . . . . . . . . . . . . . . . . . . . . . . . 37

Baalis . . . . . . . . . . . . . . . . . 24, 119
Baasha . . . . . . . . . . . . . . . . . . . . 115
Bagoas . . . . . . . . . . . . . . . . . . . . . 70
Balaam . . . . . . . 39, 87, 119–20, 124
Balak . . . . . . . . . . . . . . . . . . . . . 119
Bardiya . . . . . . . . . . . . . . . . . . . . 66
Bar-Hadad I . . . . . . . . . . . . . . . 115
Bar-Hadad II . . . . . . . . . . . 116, 117
Bata . . . . . . . . . . . . . . . . . . . . . . 48
Bathsheba . . . . . . . . . . . . . . . . . 118
Beeri . . . . . . . . . . . . . . . . . . . . . . 53
Belshazzar . . . . . . . . . . . . . . . . . 26
Ben-Hadad II . . . . . . . . . . . . . . 115
Ben-Hadad III . . . . . . . . . . . . . . 116
Beor . . . . . . . . . . . . . . . . . . . . . . 119
Berenice . . . . . . . . . . . . . . . . 76, 83
Boaz . . . . . . . . . . . . . . . . . . . . . 120

Cambyses I . . . . . . . . . . . . . . . . . 63
Cambyses II . . . . . . . . . . . . . . 66, 70
Cleopatra I . . . . . . . . . . . . . . . . . 76

Croesus . . . . . . . . . . . . . . . . . . . . 64
Cyaxares . . . . . . . . . . . . . . . . . . . 63
Cyrus II (the Great) . . . . 26, 63, 64,
66, 82, 117

Daniel . . . . . . . . . . . . . . . . . 5, 83, 84
Darius I . . . . . . . . . . . . 66, 67, 68, 69
Darius III . . . . . . . . . . . . . . . . 71, 75
David . . . . . . 20, 25, 48, 54, 88, 111,
112, 113, 114, 115, 116,
118, 120, 121, 122
Deborah . . . . . . . . . . . . . . . . 96, 109
Deliah . . . . . . . . . . . . . . . . . . . . . 70
Demetrius . . . . . . . . . . . . . . . . . . 82

Eglon . . . . . . . . . . . . . . . . . . 118, 120
Ehud . . . . . . . . . . . . . . . . . . . . . 120
Eliezer . . . . . . . . . . . . . . . . . . . . . 90
Elijah . . . . . . . . . . 93, 103, 104, 112
Elisha . . . . . . . . . 39, 87, 93, 103, 121
Elnathan . . . . . . . . . . . . . . . . . . . 68
Elon . . . . . . . . . . . . . . . . . . . . 53, 57
Ephron . . . . . . . . . . . . . . . . . . . . 53
Epicureas . . . . . . . . . . . . . . . . . . 78
Esarhaddon . . . . 20, 21, 60, 70, 118,
121, 123
Esau . . . . . . . . . . . . . . . . . 53, 91, 122
Ethbaal . . . . . . . . . . . . . . . . . . . 112
Eve . . . . . . . . . . . . . . . . . . . . . . . 15
Evil-Merodach . . . . . . . . . . . . . . 25
Ezekiel . . . . . . . . . . . . . 25, 54, 68, 87
Ezra . . . . . . . . . . 69, 71, 72, 119, 121

Gaius Popillius Laenas . . . . . . . . 80
Gedaliah . . . . . . . . . . 23, 24, 25, 119
Geshem . . . . . . . . . . . . . . . . . . . 123
Gilgamesh . . . . . . . . . . . . . . . . . 13
Goliath . . . . . . . . . . . . . . . . . . . . 48

Hadadezer . . . . . . . . . . . . . . . . 115
Hadad-idri . . . . . . . . . . . . . 115, 116
Haggai . . . . . . . . . . . . . . . . . . 67, 68
Hammurabi . . . . . . . . . . . . 7, 51, 86

Hanun . . . . . . . . . . . . . . . . . . . . 118
Hazael . . . . . . . . . . . . . . . . . . . . 116
Heliodorus . . . . . . . . . . . . 79, 82, 84
Heraclitus . . . . . . . . . . . . . . . . . . 77
Herod the Great . . . . . . . . . . . . . . 81
Herodotus . . . . . . . . . . . . . . . 19, 26
Heth . . . . . . . . . . . . . . . . . . . . . . . 53
Hezekiah . . . . . . . . . . 18, 19, 20, 22,
40, 88, 114
Hiram . . . . . . . . . . . . . . . . 111, 112
Horemheb . . . . . . . . . . . . . . . . . . 37
Hosea . . . . . . . . . . . . . . . . 103, 104
Hoshea . . . . . . . . . . . . . . . . . . . . 40
Huldah . . . . . . . . . . . . . . . . . . . . 88
Huram-abi . . . . . . . . . . . . . . . . . 112
Hyrcanus II . . . . . . . . . . . . . . . . . 81

Ibzan . . . . . . . . . . . . . . . . . . . . . . 57
Isaac . . . . . . . . . . 90, 91, 92, 101, 122
Isaiah . . . . . . . . . . . . . . . 22, 88, 103
Ishmael . . . . . . . . . . . . . . . . 24, 119
Ittobaal . . . . . . . . . . . . . . . . . . . 112

Jacob . . . . . . . . . . . 53, 56, 90, 91, 92,
99, 100, 101
Jair . . . . . . . . . . . . . . . . . . . . . . . 57
Jason . . . . . . . . . . . . . . . . 79, 80, 83
Jehoahaz . . . . . . . . . . . . . . . 22, 103
Jehoash . . . . . . . . . . . . . . . . . . . 116
Jehoiachin . . . . . . . . . . . . 22, 23, 25
Jehoiakim . . . . . . . . . . . . . . 22, 119
Jehoram . . . . . . . . . . . . 121, 122, 123
Jehoshaphat . . . . . . . . . 88, 115, 121,
122, 123
Jehu . . . . . . . . . . . . . . 16, 103, 116
Jephthah . . . . . . . . . . . . . . . . . . 118
Jeremiah . . . . . 24, 25, 39, 83, 87, 88
Jeroboam I . . . . . . . . . . . . . . . . . 40
Jeroboam II . . . . . . . . . . . . . 16, 117
Jezebel . . . . . . . . . . . . . . . . . . . 112
Joash . . . . . . . . . . . . . . . . . . . . . 116

Job . . . . . . . . . . . 3, 4, 13, 14, 47, 72,
100, 106, 107, 109
John Hyrcannus . . . . . . . . . . . . . 81
Johanan . . . . . . . . . . . . . . . . . . . 70
Jonathan . . . . . . . . . . . . . . . . . . 81
Joram . . . . . . . . . . . . . 116, 121, 123
Joseph . . . . . . . . 5, 32, 48, 49, 61, 91
Joshua . . . . . . . . . . . . 36, 66, 72, 79
Josiah . . . . . . . . . . 21, 22, 40, 88, 109
Judas Maccabeus . . . . . . . . . . 80–81

Kamose . . . . . . . . . . . . . . . . . . . 32

Laban . . . . . . . . . . . . . . . . . . 90, 91
Labashi-Marduk . . . . . . . . . . . . . 26
Lot . . . . . . . . . . . . . . . . . . 118, 119

Manasseh . . . . . . . . . . 21, 102, 103
Mandane . . . . . . . . . . . . . . . . . . 63
Manetho . . . . . . . . . . . . . . . . 31, 32
Manishtushu . . . . . . . . . . . . . . . . 2
Marduk-apla-iddina II . . . . . . . . 18
Mattathias . . . . . . . . . . . . . . . . . 80
Menelaus . . . . . . . . . . . . . . . 79, 80
Meni . . . . . . . . . . . . . . . . . . . . . . 31
Merikare . . . . . . . . . . . . . . . . . . 43
Merneptah . . . . . . . . . . . . . . 37, 38
Merodach-baladan . . . . . . . . . . . 18
Mesha . . . . . . . . . . . . . 96, 120, 122
Methuselah . . . . . . . . . . . . . . . . . 4
Micah . . . . . . . . . . . . . . . . . . . . 103
Moses . . . . . . . . . . 4, 34, 48, 59, 91,
101, 124, 125
Muwatalli II . . . . . . . . . . . . . . . . 37

Naamah . . . . . . . . . . . . . . . . . . 118
Naaman . . . . . . . . . . . . . . . . . . . 93
Nabonidus . . . . . . . . . . . 26, 64, 123
Nabopolassar . . . . . . . . . . . . . 21, 22
Nadin . . . . . . . . . . . . . . . . . . . . . 70
Nahash . . . . . . . . . . . . . . . . . . . 118
Naram-Sin . . . . . . . . . . . . . . 2, 5, 7
Nashwi . . . . . . . . . . . . . . . . . . . . 91

Nebuchadnezzar I . . . . . . . . . . . . 14
Nebuchadnezzar II . . . . . 22, 23, 25,
        26, 64, 114, 117, 121, 123
Nebuzaradan . . . . . . . . . . . . . . . . 24
Neco II . . . . . . . . . . . . . . . . . . 22, 40
Nectanebo II . . . . . . . . . . . . . . . . 31
Nehemiah . . . . 67–69, 119, 121, 124
Nergal-sharezer . . . . . . . . . . . . . . 26
Nergal-shar-usur . . . . . . . . . . . . . 26
Noah . . . . . . . . . . . . . . . . . . 4, 9, 10

Og . . . . . . . . . . . . . . . . . . . . . . . 107
Omri . . . . . . . . . . . . . . . . . 112, 120
Onias III . . . . . . . . . . . . . . . . 79, 83

Parmenides . . . . . . . . . . . . . . . . . 78
Pekah . . . . . . . . . . . . . . . . . . 17, 123
Plato . . . . . . . . . . . . . . . . . . . . . 78
Pompey . . . . . . . . . . . . . . . . . . . . 81
Potiphar . . . . . . . . . . . . . . . . 48, 61
Ptahhotep . . . . . . . . . . . . . . . 42–43
Ptolemy I . . . . . . . . . . . . . . . . . . 75
Ptolemy II . . . . . . . . . . . . . . . . . . 76
Ptolemy III . . . . . . . . . . . . . . 76, 84
Ptolemy IV . . . . . . . . . . . . . . . . . 76
Ptolemy V . . . . . . . . . . . . . . . 75, 76
Ptolemy VI . . . . . . . . . . . . . . . . . 79
Puduil . . . . . . . . . . . . . . . . . . . . 118
Pul . . . . . . . . . . . . . . . . . . . . . . . 17
Pythagoras . . . . . . . . . . . . . . . . . 78

Qoheleth . . . . . . . . . . . . . . 27, 47, 78
Queen of Kanes . . . . . . . . . . . . . . 57

Rabsaris, The . . . . . . . . . . . . . . . 19
Rabshakeh, The . . . . . . . . . . . . . . 19
Rachel . . . . . . . . . . . . . . . . . . 91, 92
Ramesses I . . . . . . . . . . . . . . . . . 37
Ramesses II . . . . . . . . . 37, 38, 49, 52
Ramesses III . . . . . . . . . . 39, 53, 113
Ramesses XI . . . . . . . . . . . . . . . . 39
Rebekah . . . . . . . . . . . . . . . . . . . 53
Rehoboam . . . . . . . . . . . . . 40, 118

Remus . . . . . . . . . . . . . . . . . . . . . 4
Reuel . . . . . . . . . . . . . . . . . . . . . 125
Rezin . . . . . . . . . . . . . . . 17, 117, 123
Rezon . . . . . . . . . . . . . . . . . . . . 115
Rib-Adda . . . . . . . . . . . . . . . . . . 36
Rimush . . . . . . . . . . . . . . . . . . . . . 2
Romulus . . . . . . . . . . . . . . . . . . . . 4
Ruth . . . . . . . . . . . . . . . . . . . . . 120

Saggil-kinam-ubbib . . . . . . . . . . 14
Samson . . . . . . . . . . . . . . . . . . . 113
Samuel . . . . . . . . . . . 39, 57, 88, 113
Sanballat . . . . . . . . . . . . . . . . 69, 70
Sanipu . . . . . . . . . . . . . . . . . . . . 118
Sarah . . . . . . . . . . . . . . . . . . . 90, 92
Sargon I (the Great) . . . . . . . 2, 4, 86
Sargon II . . 17, 18, 54, 114, 121, 123
Saul . . . . . . . 5, 6, 39, 57, 87, 88, 110,
        113, 118, 120, 122
Second Isaiah . . . . . . . . . . 25, 28, 29
Seleucus I . . . . . . . . . . . . . . . . . . 75
Seleucus IV . . . . . . . . . . . . . . 79, 82
Sennacherib . . . . . 18–20, 40, 70, 88,
        117, 118, 121, 123
Seqenenre Tao II . . . . . . . . . . . . . 32
Sethos . . . . . . . . . . . . . . . . . . . . . 19
Seti I . . . . . . . . . . . . . . . . . . . . . . 37
Shalmaneser I . . . . . . . . . . . . . 8, 90
Shalmaneser III . . . . . . 16, 111, 115,
        116, 118
Shalmaneser IV . . . . . . . . . . . . . 117
Shalmaneser V . . . . . . . . . . . . . . 17
Shamash-shuma-ukin . . . . . . . . . 21
Shamgar ben Anat . . . . . . . 109, 113
Shamshi-Adad I . . . . . . . . . . . . . . 7
Shaphan . . . . . . . . . . . . . . . . . . . 24
Sharezer . . . . . . . . . . . . . . . . . . . 20
Shar-kali-sharri . . . . . . . . . . . . . . 2
Sharru-kin . . . . . . . . . . . . . . . . . . 2
Shealtiel . . . . . . . . . . . . . . . . . . . 67
Shelemiah . . . . . . . . . . . . . . . . . . 70
Sheshbazzar . . . . . . . . . . . . . 65, 66
Sheshonq I . . . . . . . . . . . . . . . . . 40

Shishak . . . . . . . . . . . . . . . . . . . . . 40
Shobi . . . . . . . . . . . . . . . . . . . . . 118
Shubshi-meshre-Shakkan . . 13–14
Sihon . . . . . . . . . . . . . . . . . . . . . 119
Simon . . . . . . . . . . . . . . . . . . . . 81
Sin-shar-ishkun . . . . . . . . . . . . . . 21
Sin-shumu-lishir . . . . . . . . . . . . . 21
Sinuhe . . . . . . . . . . . . . . . . . . . . . 48
Smenkhkare . . . . . . . . . . . . . . . . 34
So . . . . . . . . . . . . . . . . . . . . . . . . 40
Socrates . . . . . . . . . . . . . . . . . . . . 78
Solomon . . . . . 40, 54, 109, 112, 114,
                115, 118, 120, 122
Suppiluliuma . . . . . . . . . . . . . . . 52

Taharqa . . . . . . . . . . . . . . . . . 19, 20
Tartan, The . . . . . . . . . . . . . . . . . 19
Thutmose I . . . . . . . . . . . . . . . . . 33
Thutmose III . . . . . . . . . . . . . . . . 33
Thutmose IV . . . . . . . . . . . . . 33, 90
Tiglath-pileser I . . . . . . . . . . . . . 111
Tiglath-pileser III . . . . . 16, 17, 111,
                114, 117, 118, 121, 123
Tirhakah . . . . . . . . . . . . . . . . . . . 19
Tobiah . . . . . . . . . . . . . . . . . . . . 119
Tobit . . . . . . . . . . . . . . . . . . . . . . 70
Tola . . . . . . . . . . . . . . . . . . . . . . . 57

Tudhaliya II . . . . . . . . . . . . . . . . . 52
Tudhaliya III . . . . . . . . . . . . . . . . 52
Tukulti-Ninurta I . . . . . . . . . . . . . . 8
Tutankhamun . . . . . . . . . 34, 37, 52
Tutankhaten . . . . . . . . . . . . . . . . 34

Uriah . . . . . . . . . . . . . . . . . . . . . 118
Utnapishtim . . . . . . . . . . . . . . . . . 9
Utu-kegal . . . . . . . . . . . . . . . . . . . 3
Uzziah . . . . . . . . . . . . . . . . . . . . 123

Wen-Amun . . . . . . . . . . . . . 39, 111
Wullu . . . . . . . . . . . . . . . . . . . . . 91

Xerxes I . . . . . . . . . . . . . . . . . 68, 72

Yehoezer . . . . . . . . . . . . . . . . . . . 68

Zadok . . . . . . . . . . . . . . . . . . . . . 79
Zannanza . . . . . . . . . . . . . . . . . . 52
Zechariah . . . . . . . . . . . . . . . . 56, 67
Zedekiah . . . . . . . . . . . . 22, 88, 123
Zerah . . . . . . . . . . . . . . . . . . . . . . 40
Zerkarbaal . . . . . . . . . . . . . . . . . 39
Zerubbabel . . . . . . . . . . . . . . 66, 67
Zimri-lim . . . . . . . . . . . . . . . . . . 86
Ziusudra . . . . . . . . . . . . . . . . . . . . 4
Zohar . . . . . . . . . . . . . . . . . . . . . . 53

# Index of Locations

"Across the River" .......... 68
Aegean .......... 39, 53, 113, 114
Agade ..................... 64
Akhetaten ................. 33
Akka ..................... 111
Akkad ................. 2, 5, 64
Alalakh ................... 15
Alaouite Mountains ......... 94
Aleppo ........... 37, 85, 89, 93
Alexandria .............. 77, 80
Ammon ....... 24, 118, 119, 121,
                            122, 123
Amurru ................. 36, 37
Anathoth .................. 108
Anatolia ...... 8, 33, 51, 52, 53, 63,
                            79, 89
Aphek ................. 115, 116
Arabah Valley ............. 121
Arabia ............. 26, 118, 119
Aradus ................... 111
Aram .............. 115–17, 123
Arnon River ........... 118, 119
Ashdod ........... 113, 114, 121
Ashkelon ................. 38, 113
Ashshur ........... 7, 21, 63, 64

Asia Minor .............. 64, 71
Assyria ..... 7, 8, 12, 16, 17, 18, 20,
              21, 22, 40, 63, 75, 89, 90
                111, 117, 118, 122
Aswan ..................... 70
Avaris .................... 32
Avva ..................... 17
Azekah ................... 24

Babel .................... 4, 27
Babylon ... 7, 17, 18, 20, 21, 22, 24,
          26, 27, 40, 51, 56, 64, 65, 66, 67,
      69, 75, 76, 86, 89, 106, 119, 122, 123
Babylonia .... 1, 7, 8, 12, 16, 17, 18,
          21, 22, 23, 26, 64, 82, 84, 121, 123
Bashan .................... 107
Beth-Anat ................. 108
Beth-Anoth ................ 108
Bethel ............... 87, 99, 100
Bethlehem ................. 57
Beth-shan .......... 109, 110, 115
Black Sea .................. 66
Bogazköy ............. 51, 60, 99
Byblos ............... 36, 39, 111

Canaan . . . 36, 37, 38, 39, 53, 54, 91,
    92, 97, 107, 118, 119, 122, 125
Carchemish . . . . . . . . . . . 22, 53, 93
Chebar River . . . . . . . . . . . . . . . 23
Cuthah . . . . . . . . . . . . . . . . . . . . 17
Cyprus . . . . . . . . . . . . . . . . . . . . 68

Damascus . . . . 16, 17, 115, 116, 117
Dead Sea . . . . . . . . . . . . . . 119, 121
Deir Alla . . . . . . . . . . . . . . 119–20
Der . . . . . . . . . . . . . . . . . . . . . . . 64

Ebenezer . . . . . . . . . . . . . . . . . . 113
Ebla . . . . . . . . . . . . . . 85–86, 89, 93
Eden . . . . . . . . . . . . . . . . . . . . . . 15
Edom . . . . . . . . . 24, 90, 121–24, 125
Egypt . . . 4, 8, 20, 21, 22, 24, 25, 31,
    32, 33, 36, 38, 39, 40, 43, 47, 48,
    52, 53, 54, 58, 66, 68, 69, 70, 71,
    75, 76, 79, 80, 84, 86, 89, 106,
    112, 113, 114, 121, 122, 124
Ekron . . . . . . . . . . . . . 113, 114, 115
Elam . . . . . . . . . . . . . . . . . . . 18, 21
el-Amarna . . . . . . . . . . . . . 33, 34, 36
Elath . . . . . . . . . . . . . . . . . . . . . 123
Elephantine . . . 25, 70, 71, 109, 117
Eltekeh . . . . . . . . . . . . . . . . . . . . 18
Emar . . . . . . . . . . . . . . . 89, 93–94
Eridu . . . . . . . . . . . . . . . . . . . . . . 5
Eshnunna . . . . . . . . . . . 7, 10, 11, 64
Euphrates River . . . . 1, 6, 33, 54, 93
Euphrates Valley . . . . . . . . . . . . . 86

Galilee . . . . . . . . . . . . . . . . . . 17, 21
Gath . . . . . . . . . . . . . . 113, 114, 116
Gaza . . . . . . . . . 17, 71, 76, 113, 114
Gezer . . . . . . . . . . . . . . . . . . . . . . 38
Gihon Spring . . . . . . . . . . . . . . . 18
Gilead . . . . . . . . . . . . . . . 17, 21, 57
Greece . . . . . . 40, 66, 68, 75, 79, 83,
    114, 121
Gulf of Aqaba . . 121, 123, 124, 125
Gutium . . . . . . . . . . . . . . . . . . . . 64

Hamath . . . . . . . . . . . 17, 53, 54, 117
Harran . . . . . . . . . . . . . . . . . . . . . 22
Hatti . . . . . . . . 36, 37, 51, 52, 53, 54
Hattusa . . . . . . . . . . . . . . . . . 51, 52
Hazor . . . . . . . . . . . . . . . . . . . . . . 5
Heshbon . . . . . . . . . . . . . . . . . . 119
Horeb . . . . . . . . . . . . . . . . . . . . 124
Hurru . . . . . . . . . . . . . . . . . 38, 122

Idumea . . . . . . . . . . . . . . . . . . . . 81
India . . . . . . . . . . . . . . . . . . . . 1, 64
Indus River . . . . . . . . . . . . . . 71, 75
Iran . . . . . . . . . . . . . . . . . . 1, 21, 63
Iraq . . . . . . . . . . . . . . . . . . 1, 86, 90
Isin . . . . . . . . . . . . . . . . . . . . . . 6, 7
Israel . . . . . 3, 5, 9, 10, 16, 17, 20, 25
    31, 36, 37, 38, 39, 40, 54, 64, 71
    75, 85, 86, 88, 93, 95, 96, 100,
    101, 102, 103, 104, 108, 111,
    112, 114, 115, 116, 117, 118,
    119, 122, 124, 125
Istanbul . . . . . . . . . . . . . . . . . . . 18

Jabbok River . . . . . . . . . . . . 56, 118
Jabesh-Gilead . . . . . . . . . . . . . . 118
Jable . . . . . . . . . . . . . . . . . . . . . . 94
Jebel el-Aqra . . . . . . . . . . . . . 94, 96
Jerusalem . . . . . 5, 15, 16, 18, 19, 22,
    23, 24, 36, 40, 54, 64, 65, 67, 68,
    69, 70, 71, 76, 77, 78, 79, 80, 81,
    88, 96, 102, 107, 112, 114, 116,
    117, 118, 119, 121, 123, 124, 125
Jordan . . . . . . . . . . . . . . . . . . 24, 119
Jordan River . . 24, 93, 116, 118, 119
Judah . . 9, 17, 18, 19, 20, 21, 22, 23,
    26, 56, 64, 65, 66, 67, 68, 69, 70,
    71, 75, 87, 96, 102, 103, 107,
    115, 116, 117, 119, 121, 123
Judea . . 24, 76, 78, 79, 80, 81, 82, 84

Kadesh-Barnea . . . . . . . . . . . . . . 103
Kanes . . . . . . . . . . . . . . . . . . . . . . 57
Karnak . . . . . . . . . . . . . . . . . 38, 40

Khatana-Qantir .............. 37
Khirbet-el-Qom ............. 103
Khorsabad ................. 114
Kirkuk ..................... 90
Kish ........................ 2
Kuntillet Ajrûd ......... 103, 125

Lachish .............. 18, 19, 24
Lagash ...................... 2
Larsa ..................... 6, 7
Lebanon .......... 7, 33, 54, 110
Lebanon Mountains ........ 110
Luash ..................... 117
Lydia ................... 26, 64

Macedonia ................. 71
Machpelah ................. 53
Magnesia .................. 79
Marathon .................. 66
Mari ............. 7, 86, 88, 89, 93
Medeba ................... 120
Media ............... 26, 63, 82
Mediterranean .... 2, 8, 16, 33, 39,
     53, 69, 86, 94, 96, 110, 111, 112
Megiddo ................. 22, 33
Memphis .............. 20, 21, 25
Mesopotamia ... 1, 2, 3, 6, 7, 8, 10,
     14, 17, 18, 22, 31, 33, 36,
     65, 69, 86, 89, 94, 110, 114
Me-Turnu .................. 64
Midian ................. 124–25
Migdol ..................... 25
Minet el-Beida .............. 94
Mitanni ............. 8, 33, 36, 52,
     89–90, 94, 122
Mizpah .................... 24
Moab .......... 96, 118, 119–21,
     122, 123, 124
Modein .................... 80
Mount Carmel .... 16, 87, 104, 112
Mount Gilboa ............. 113
Mount Paran .............. 125
Mount Sinai ........ 105, 124, 125

Mount Zaphon .......... 96, 107
Mount Zion ........ 22, 25, 96, 97

Nile River .......... 4, 35, 37, 70
Nineveh .............. 19, 21, 63
Nippur .................. 5, 66
Nuzi ........... 90, 91, 92, 93, 94

Opis ....................... 64
Orontes River .......... 16, 33, 37

Palestine ..... 32, 33, 69, 75, 76, 77
     78, 82, 84, 114
Paran .................... 125
Peor ................... 120, 124
Persepolis .................. 75
Persia .......... 40, 63, 66, 68, 71,
     83, 114, 117, 121
Persian Gulf ................. 1
Philistia ............ 18, 112, 114
Phoenicia ...... 16, 68, 69, 110–11
Piramesses ................. 37
Pirathon .................. 57
Pithom .................... 37

Qadesh .............. 33, 37, 54
Qarqar .......... 16, 115, 116, 118

Rabbah ................... 118
Ramoth-Gilead ... 20, 88, 115, 116
Raphia .................... 76
Ras Shamra ................ 94
Reuel .................... 125
Rome ............. 4, 80, 81, 114

Samaria ..... 17, 21, 24, 54, 69, 70,
     78, 103, 115, 125
Scythia .................... 66
Seir ............. 90, 122, 124, 125
Sepharvaim ................ 17
Shechem .................. 100
Shittim ................... 124
Sidon ........ 16, 20, 109, 111, 112

Sinai Peninsula ......... 103, 125
Sumer ................... 5, 64
Susa .................... 64, 75
Syria .... 6, 8, 15, 16, 17, 33, 36, 51,
52, 53, 54, 63, 66, 68, 71,
75, 85, 86, 89, 94, 97, 115
Syro-Palestine ......... 33, 36, 48,
70, 75, 85

Tabqa Dam ................. 93
Tahpanhes ................. 25
Tarsus .................... 79
Tehran .................... 63
Teima .................... 26
Tekoa .................... 96
Tel Dan .............. 116, 121
Tell Hariri ................ 86
Tell Mardikh ............. 85
Tell Meskene ............. 93
Teman ................ 103, 125
Thebes ............... 21, 32, 34
Tigris River ............ 1, 64, 90
Timna .................... 125

Tyre .. 16, 20, 71, 104, 111, 112, 117

Ugarit ..... 8, 39, 60, 86, 89, 94, 96,
97, 98, 99, 100, 101, 105, 106,
107, 108, 109, 110
Ur ................. 2, 3, 5, 6, 26
Urartu .................... 16
Uruk .................... 2, 5

Valley of Rephaim ........... 114

Wadi-Hasa ............. 119, 121
Wadi Mujib ........... 118, 119

Yahu .................... 125
Yanoam ................... 38
Yarkon River .............. 112
Yehud ................. 66, 68

Zagros Mountains ............. 3
Zamban ................... 64
Zarqa River .............. 118
Zered River .......... 119, 121
Zobah ................... 115

CPSIA information can be obtained at www.ICGtesting.com
Printed in the USA
LVOW130002171012

303084LV00002B/2/P